THE
PREMIERSHIP
FOOTBALL
MISCELLANY

I would like to dedicate this book to my wife, Janice, and our two sons, Marc and Paul.

First published in 2008
Second edition 2013
Carlton Books Limited
20 Mortimer Street
London W1T 3JW

A CIP catalogue record for this book is available from the British Library

ISBN: 978-1-78097-378-4

Editor: Martin Corteel
Assistant Editor: David Ballheimer
Project Art Editor: Darren Jordan
Production: Janette Burgin

Printed and bound by CPI Group (UK) Ltd, Croydon, CR0 4YY

THE PREMIERSHIP FOOTBALL MISCELLANY

WITH A FOREWORD BY
SIR ALEX FERGUSON, CBE

SECOND EDITION

JOHN WHITE

CARLTON
BOOKS

～ **FOREWORD BY SIR ALEX FERGUSON** ～

I feel extremely privileged to have been a manager in the Premier League since its inaugural season in 1992–93 and even more privileged to have managed in it until May 2013. The Premier League is without question the most attractive and toughest football league in the world. This is not to say that France's Ligue 1, Germany's Bundesliga, Italy's Serie A, Holland's Eredivisie, Spain's La Liga or indeed Brazil's Campeonato Série A or Argentina's Primera División are easy to win, they are just not as demanding or intense over the course of their respective seasons. Some will argue why then a Premiership club does not win the UEFA Champions League year in and year out, which is a valid point, but I just feel that our 38-game season, coupled with Carling Cup, FA Cup and international matches, is the ultimate test of a team's strengths and weaknesses.

Few would disagree when I say that history has shown that the best team in the UEFA Champions League does not always collect Europe's most coveted club prize at the end of a season, whereas the fact remains that the best team over the course of the season will always win the equally coveted Premier League title. Indeed, one only has to look at the vast array of international superstars who currently grace our Premiership: players such as Germany's Lukas Podolski at Arsenal, Argentina's Carlos Tevez at Manchester City, the Czech Republic's Petr Cech, Brazil's Davild Luiz and Spain's Fernando Torres at Chelsea, and England's Steven Gerrard and Uruguay's Luis Suarez at Liverpool, as well as England's Wayne Rooney, Wales's Ryan Giggs and Holland's Robin van Persie at Manchester United to see that the Premier League is not just a league where some of the world's best managers want to manage, but also the league where some of the world's best footballers want to test their skills week in and week out.

Since its inception in the 1992–93 season the Premier League has over the last 21 seasons attracted many players who are now quite rightly accredited legendary status. Players with outstanding abilities, mercurial skill, magnificent talent and the odd sprinkling of "genius" have entertained millions of fans up and down the country. There are far too many to list in total, but by way of a fond reminder here are just a few: David Beckham , Dennis Bergkamp, Eric Cantona, Robbie Fowler, Thierry Henry, Juninho, Jurgen Klinsmann, Michael Owen, Peter Schmeichel, Alan Shearer and Gianfranco Zola. Every one of these truly gifted footballers have all left their individual mark in one way or another in the annals of Premiership history, while many from the modern era will no doubt join them.

In closing, I hope John's book will help rekindle many of your own fond memories of outstanding achievements by your own team since the Premiership began, but also provide you with the occasional "I forgot about that" as you leaf through the book page-by-page while at the same time being taken on a wonderful journey covering all that is mystical about this truly wonderful league. Naturally, there is the odd near miss or two thrown into the mix, but then that is football – a game of fantastic highs and lows. Happy reading.

Sir Alex Ferguson, CBE

~ ACKNOWLEDGEMENTS ~

Before you commence reading this book, I would like to take the opportunity to pay tribute to all those people who helped me finalise my book into the volume you now hold in your hands.

I would like to personally thank a number of very deserving people, both family and friends: Davy Campbell, Bill Clarkson, Addy Dearnaley, John and Martin Dempsey, Frankie Dodds (aka Dodger), Marty Ferguson, Damien Friel (aka Big Dee), Mickey Morrison, Bobby and Ruth McWilliams my father-in-law and mother-in-law, my own mum Rosaleen Doherty White, my brother David and sisters Danielle, Donna and Michelle.

Thanks also to my publishers and in particular Martin Corteel at Carlton Publishing Limited. Martin and I have collaborated on a dozen projects and we have formed a good team. Martin, I fully appreciate all that you have done for me.

And to my wife Janice and our sons Marc and Paul – you know I could not have done this without you.

However, there is one very special person who is no longer with us that I must pay tribute to, my father John McDermot White. My dad was the leading light behind my love of football and still shines his light brightly on me today.

Miss You Dad

John

⊸◦ INTRODUCTION ◦⊸

What can I possibly say about the greatest football league in the world that Sir Alex Ferguson hasn't already mentioned? I am sure the Boss will not mind me pinching his own famous line after Manchester United beat FC Bayern Munich at Camp Nou on 29 May 1999 to win the UEFA Champions League and with it the unprecedented treble alongside the Premier League crown and FA Cup: "Football, Bloody Hell!" Having watched countless Premiership games since the inaugural season kicked off in 1992–93, I now know just what Sir Alex meant when he uttered that memorable line.

Football is a game of highs and lows, or "two halves" as the legendary Jimmy Greaves once said. One minute you can be cheering your team on to victory only to see the game turn around in the closing minutes and ecstasy turns to agony as late goals scupper your plans of celebrating the evening. I for one know that I have been in a foul mood, felt down or simply put off my food because my own team, Manchester United, did not win, and I know fans of the other 45 clubs that have played in the Premiership up to the end of the 2012–13 season, will recognize this malaise.

The legendary Bill Shankly once quipped: "Some people believe football is a matter of life and death. I'm very disappointed with that attitude. I can assure you it is much, much more important than that." For many fans Shanks' words ring true in that they live for their football and support their team passionately until the day they die.

Football has always played a huge part of my life from the moment I first saw a young George Best glide across our television screen at home in Belfast as he helped Manchester United to victory in the 1968 European Cup final. From that moment on I was hooked on the Belfast Boy and United and covered my room in posters from *Shoot!* magazine and made sure my mum bought Cookstown sausages for tea. Naturally, I had to have a pair of Bestie's Stylo football boots (although admittedly they never made me play like him!) and I even attended a secondary school in Belfast whose primary uniform colours were red, white and black!

I am extremely passionate about my football and am quite privileged to say that this is my 16th published title on the game I love. I hope you enjoy reading my book and that it helps brings back many fond memories you have from watching your own team grace the greatest football league in the world, the Premier League.

John White
June 2013

☙ FINAL PREMIERSHIP TABLE 1992–93 ☙

Pos Team	P	W	D	L	F	A	Pts
1. Manchester United (C)	42	24	12	6	67	31	84
2. Aston Villa	42	21	11	10	57	40	74
3. Norwich City	42	21	9	12	61	65	72
4. Blackburn Rovers	42	20	11	11	68	46	71
5. Queen's Park Rangers	42	17	12	13	63	55	63
6. Liverpool	42	16	11	15	62	55	59
7. Sheffield Wednesday	42	15	14	13	55	51	59
8. Tottenham Hotspur	42	16	11	15	60	66	59
9. Manchester City	42	15	12	15	56	51	57
10. Arsenal	42	15	11	16	40	38	56
11. Chelsea	42	14	14	14	51	54	56
12. Wimbledon	42	14	12	16	56	55	54
13. Everton	42	15	8	19	53	55	53
14. Sheffield United	42	14	10	18	54	53	52
15. Coventry City	42	13	13	16	52	57	52
16. Ipswich Town	42	12	16	14	50	55	52
17. Leeds United	42	12	15	15	57	62	51
18. Southampton	42	13	11	18	54	61	50
19. Oldham Athletic	42	13	10	19	63	74	49
20. Crystal Palace (R)	42	11	16	15	48	61	49
21. Middlesbrough (R)	42	11	11	20	54	75	44
22. Nottingham Forest (R)	42	10	10	22	41	62	40

☙ BORO JOY ☙

Of the three clubs promoted to the Premier League at the end of the 1997–98 season (Charlton Athletic, Middlesbrough and Nottingham Forest) only Middlesbrough avoided an immediate drop into the First Division. Boro finished a highly respectable ninth. It was their highest league finish for more than 20 years.

☙ MARCHING TO A NEW TROT ☙

On 25 October 2007, Bolton Wanderers unveiled their latest signing – new manager Gary Megson, who left Leicester City to take charge of the Trotters following Sammy Lee's sacking. Bolton lay at the foot of the Premiership table with just five points from their opening ten games. "Gary has demonstrated he has the right temperament for a battle, which this season is undoubtedly going to be," said Phil Gartside, the Bolton chairman.

❧ FORMATION OF THE FA PREMIER LEAGUE ❦

As the 1987–88 season began, the Football League was planning how to celebrate the centenary of its formation in 1888. Such plans were soon overshadowed, however, by a threat from ten of the leading teams at the time, most notably Arsenal, Liverpool and Manchester United, to break away from their controlling body and form a new elite Super League that would generative lucrative television money for the clubs concerned.

Matters came to a head in 1991 when the Football Association unveiled its new master plan (*"Blueprint for Football"*) in which the idea of a new Super League to comprise the top 18 clubs at the time was mooted. On 14 June 1991, 16 English First Division clubs began the process of severing their ties with the Football League by putting their names to a document of intent to join a new league, to be known as the FA Premier League. Soon afterwards the remaining six First Division clubs jumped ship and all 22 tendered their resignation from the Football League. On 20 February 1992 the FA Premier League, commercially independent of the Football Association and the Football League, was officially formed. The 1991–92 season ended with Leeds United pipping Manchester United to be crowned the last ever champions of the old First Division. The following season, 1992–93, Manchester United won the inaugural FA Premier League (FAPL), their first championship success in 26 years.

❧ THE JEWEL IN THE CROWN ❦

During the 1999–2000 season Manchester United withdrew from the FA Cup at the request of the Football Association so that they could participate in the inaugural FIFA World Club Championship. The FA wanted the jewel of English football's crown to play in Brazil in an effort to help bolster England's chances of hosting the 2006 FIFA World Cup finals. It was the first time in the history of the competition that the reiging FA Cup holders chose not to defend the famous trophy, and while United's Premiership opponents were slogging it out on rock-hard pitches up and down England the United players were basking in the sunshine in Rio de Janeiro.

❧ DEADLY DOUG DEPARTS ❦

On 19 September 2006, Randy Lerner replaced 82-year-old Doug Ellis as the chairman of Aston Villa.

❧ PREMIERSHIP TALK (1) ❧

"When the seagulls follow the trawler, it is because they think sardines will be thrown into the sea."
Eric Cantona (Manchester United), February 1995

❧ FA CHANGES PREMIER LEAGUE RULES ❧

The Football Association introduced a cap of 25 players to be registered in a Premier League squad from the closure of the transfer window in August 2010. However, players aged 21 and under did not have to be in the 25 and could still be selected. Another new rule – on home-grown players – required clubs to have at least eight players in their 25-man squad who had been registered domestically for at least three seasons prior to their 21st birthday.

❧ YOUNG BIRDS AND OLD POTTERS ❧

Norwich City had the youngest average age for a squad in the Premier League during season 2011–12, 25.08 years. Stoke City had the oldest at 28.42 years.

❧ THE BATTLE OF THE BUFFET TABLE ❧

On 24 October 2004, Manchester United ended Arsenal's record 49-game unbeaten run in the top flight with a 2–0 win at Old Trafford. After the game a scuffle broke out between players from both teams, which spread to the changing-room area, with slices of pizza and even pea soup being thrown at Sir Alex Ferguson and several of the Manchester United players. This led to the game being dubbed "The Battle of the Buffet" and resulted in an even more intense and bitter rivalry between the two sides. In the return game at Highbury on 1 February 2005, Roy Keane and Patrick Vieira clashed in the tunnel before kick-off, and Mikael Silvestre was sent off during the game for head-butting Freddie Ljungberg. Despite only having ten men, United won 4–2 to complete a treble over Arsenal, having also knocked them out of the League Cup earlier in the season.

❧ ARSENE HONOURED ❧

In 2002 Arsene Wenger, the manager of Arsenal, was awarded France's highest decoration, the Legion d'Honneur.

❧ THE MAGNIFICENT SEVEN ❧

Since the inception of the Premier League in season 1992–93, only seven teams have played every season of the league's 21-year history (includes season 2012–13):

❧ Arsenal ❧
❧ Aston Villa ❧
❧ Chelsea ❧
❧ Everton ❧
❧ Liverpool ❧
❧ Manchester United ❧
❧ Tottenham Hotspur ❧

❧ BLUES HAT-TRICK ❧

In season 2005–06, which marked Chelsea's 101st campaign, the Blues won their second successive Premier League title. It was the third championship success in the club's history.

❧ STICKY TOFFEE ESCAPE ❧

On the final day of the 1993-94 season Everton, league champions seven years earlier, were in danger of being relegated from the Premiership. Things were going badly for the Toffees when they trailed Wimbledon 2–0 at half-time at Goodison Park. However, with top-flight football for the following season under threat, Everton turned the game, and their fortunes, around in the second half, scoring three times to win 3–2 and stay up. Swindon Town were already relegated going into the final day, and the remaining two relegation places went to Oldham Athletic, who failed to beat Norwich City (ironically the team the Everton manager Mike Walker had managed for the first five months of the season), and Sheffield United, who lost to Chelsea.

❧ 129-YEAR-OLD DEFENCE ❧

Lee Dixon (38), Tony Adams (35), Martin Keown (35) and Ashley Cole (21) were the Arsenal back four that helped the club achieve the domestic Double in season 2001–02. Behind them in goal was 38-year-old David Seaman. They leaked just 36 goals between them in the 38 Premiership games played and were the second meanest defence behind the Liverpool back four, who only conceded 30 goals.

❧ DAVID BECKHAM, OBE ❧

David Robert Joseph Beckham was born on 2 May 1975 in Leytonstone, London. In 1989 he signed schoolboy forms with Manchester United, became a trainee in July 1991 and, on 23 September 1992, made his United debut in a Rumbelows Cup tie at Brighton & Hove Albion. In May 1996, a Beckham-inspired United became the first English club to win the coveted Double twice following their all-conquering 1993–94 season. On the opening day of the 1996–97 season, David scored perhaps the greatest Premier League goal of all time when he sensationally chipped Neil Sullivan of Wimbledon from 55 yards.

On 1 September 1996, David made his full England debut in a 3–0 World Cup qualifying victory away to Moldova. However, during the 1998 World Cup finals in France, he was sent off against Argentina and England lost in a penalty shoot-out. Many fans and journalists blamed him for England's elimination and he became the target of severe criticism and abuse, but Beckham was undaunted and in 1999 he inspired United to the treble of Premier League, FA Cup and UEFA Champions League. In October 2000, England caretaker manager Peter Taylor appointed David captain, a role he relished. On 6 October 2001, he almost single-handedly ensured England reached the 2002 World Cup finals. In their final qualifying game, needing only a draw, England were trailing Greece 2–1 at Old Trafford with just seconds remaining. Beckham stepped up to fire home an injury-time equaliser to book England's trip to Japan and Korea. Beckham avenged England's 1998 loss to Argentina by scoring from the penalty spot to give his side a 1–0 win in Sapporo, Japan.

After helping United to an eighth Premier League title in 2002–03, David joined Real Madrid. It took David four seasons to finally win a champions medal in Spain, helping Real Madrid to the 2006–07 La Liga title. It was his Spanish swansong, as he had already signed to play for the Los Angeles Galaxy in Major League Soccer. His arrival in the United States caused a firestorm of interest, but, again, it took him four years to win MLS title. David's dream of playing in a fourth World Cup in South Africa in 2010 were dashed by an achilles tendon rupture whilst on loan with AC Milan in March that year, and he finished his international career with 115 caps and 17 goals. After winning a second MLS title in late 2012, David returned to Europe and joined French giants Paris Saint-Germain in February 2013. He retired at the end of the season.

Did You Know That?
On 12 November 2005, David captained England for the 50th time, during their 3–2 friendly win over Argentina in Geneva, Switzerland.

⚔ SKY FALLS IN ON SKY BLUES ⚔

In season 2000–01 Coventry City's luck finally ran out when the Sky Blues lost their top-flight status after 34 consecutive years among the big boys. During the 34 years their highest league placing was sixth.

⚔ CANNIBAL RACIST REMARK ⚔

After helping Nottingham Forest to the First Division Championship title in season 1997–98, and a return to the Premiership, Kevin Campbell left Forest and joined Trabzonspor in Turkey. However, he only stayed with the Istanbul-based club for seven months and left them for Everton following a racist incident involving the club's president, Mehmet Ali Yilmaz, who called Campbell a "discoloured cannibal" and also said about the striker: "We bought him as a goal machine, but he appeared to be a washing machine." In March 1999 he signed for Everton on loan and scored nine Premiership goals in eight games for the Toffees, making him the Goodison Park outfit's leading goalscorer in season 1998–99, despite the fact that he had been at the club for less than four weeks. In the summer of 1999 Campbell signed for Everton on a permanent deal worth £3 million.

⚔ A SAINTLY DEPARTURE ⚔

At the end of the 1996–97 season Graeme Souness, the manager of Southampton, quit his position at The Dell after just one season at the helm and was replaced by Dave Jones from Stockport County. Souness had won the Premier League Manager of the Month Award for April 1997.

⚔ TROUBLE DOWN THE LANE ⚔

On 25 October 2007, Tottenham Hotspur sacked their manager Martin Jol just hours prior to kick-off of what proved to be a disappointing 2–1 home loss to Getafe in the UEFA Cup. Three days later Spurs replaced Jol with the Seville manager Juande Ramos and brought in former White Hart Lane favourite Gus Poyet from Leeds United to act as first-team coach under Ramos. A few days after Jol's sacking, Daniel Levy, the Tottenham chairman, admitted the club made mistakes with the departure of Jol. Much to the embarrassment of Spurs, the news that Jol had been fired was leaked before the game and spread to media and fans as the match against Getafe went on.

❧ FA PREMIER LEAGUE CLUBS 1992–2013 ❧

Club	Seasons in FAPL	Spells in FAPL	Most recent FAPL season	FAPL seasons
Arsenal*	21	1	2012–13	Ever present
Aston Villa*	21	1	2012–13	Ever present
Barnsley	1	1	1997–98	1997–98
Birmingham City	9	2	2010–11	2002–06, 2007–08 2009–11
Blackpool	1	1	2010–11	2010–11
Blackburn Rovers*	18	2	2011–12	1992–99, 2001–12
Bolton Wanderers	13	3	2011–12	1995–96, 1997–98 2001–12
Bradford City	2	1	2000–01	1999–2001
Burnley	1	1	2009–10	2009–10
Charlton Athletic	8	2	2006–07	1998–99, 2000–07
Chelsea*	21	1	2012–13	Ever present
Coventry City*	9	1	2000–01	1992–2001
Crystal Palace*	4	4	2004–05	1992–93, 1994–95 1997–98, 2004–05
Derby County	6	2	2007–08	1996–2002, 2007–08
Everton*	21	1	2012–13	Ever present
Fulham	12	1	2012–13	2001–present
Hull City	2	1	2009–10	2008–10
Ipswich Town*	5	2	2001–02	1992–95, 2000–02
Leeds United*	12	1	2003–04	1992–2004
Leicester City	8	3	2003–04	1994–95, 1996–2002 2003–04
Liverpool*	21	1	2012–13	Ever present
Manchester City*	15	2	2012–13	1992–96, 2002–present
Manchester Utd*	21	1	2012–13	Ever present
Middlesbrough*	14	3	2008–09	1992–93, 1995–97 1998–2009
Newcastle United	18	2	2012–13	1993–2009, 2011–
Norwich City*	6	3	2012–13	1992–95, 2004–05, 2011–
Nottingham Forest*	5	3	1998–99	1992–93, 1994–97 1998–99
Oldham Athletic*	2	1	1993–94	1992–94
Portsmouth	7	1	2009–10	2003–10
QPR*	6	2	2012–13	1992–96, 2011–
Reading	3	2	2012–13	2006–08, 2012–
Sheffield United*	3	2	2006–07	1992–94, 2006–07

Sheffield Wed*	8	1	1999–2000	1992–2000
Southampton*	14	2	2012–13	1992–2005
				2012–
Stoke City	5	1	2012–13	2008–
Sunderland	6	3	2007–08	1996–97, 1999–2003
				2005–06, 2007–
Swansea City	2	1	2012–13	2011–
Swindon Town	1	1	1993–94	1993–94
Tottenham Hotspur*	21	1	2012–13	Ever present
Watford	2	2	2006–07	1999–2000, 2006–07
WBA	7	4	2012–13	2002–03, 2004–06
				2008–09, 2010–
West Ham United	13	4	2012–13	1993–2003,
				2005–11, 2012–
Wigan Athletic	8	1	2012–13	2005–present
Wimbledon*	8	1	1999–2000	1992–2000
Wolves	4	2	2011–12	2003–04, 2009–12

* *Teams in the inaugural Premier League season of 1992–93 (22 clubs).*

Teams in bold were 2012–13 Premier League sides (20 clubs).

Did You Know That
Aston Villa are the only ever-present club not to have played in the UEFA Champions League since it was rebranded in 1992.

❧ THE SAS ❧

At the end of 1993–94, Norwich City's Chris Sutton left Carrow Road to join Kenny Dalglish's resurgent Blackburn Rovers, Premiership runners-up to Manchester United, for an English club record fee of £5 million. Sutton would line up alongside Alan Shearer for the 1994–95 season, as the Ewood Park club sought to end their 81-year wait for a League title, and the pair were nicknamed the SAS.

❧ TWINKLE TOES ❧

When Glenn Hoddle moved to Chelsea at the start of the 1993–94 season he became the first player-manager in Premier League history. The former Spurs, AS Monaco and England player secured the first European football for the Blues in 20 years when they qualified for the European Cup Winners' Cup, despite losing the 1994 FA Cup final to the Double winners, Manchester United.

✂ PREMIERSHIP TALK (2) ✂

"But, at the moment, when I step on the pitch, when I have the ball I know it's mine. It's just a feeling."
Thierry Henry (Arsenal)

✂ DOZY PLAYER ✂

On 6 February 2008, Portsmouth's chief executive Peter Storrie stated that Benjani Mwaruwari's transfer to Manchester City failed to take place on transfer deadline day (31 January 2008) because the player fell asleep when he was supposed to be catching an airplane to the north-west. As Storrie put it: "In his own inevitable, wonderful way – and we all love Benji so much – he falls asleep at the airport and misses two planes." In the end Benjani was permitted to join Manchester City two days past the deadline.

✂ UNITED STOP ARSENAL FA CUP TREBLE ✂

In season 2003–04 Manchester United prevented Arsenal from reaching their third consecutive FA Cup final by defeating the 2002 and 2003 FA Cup winners in the semi-final. United went on to beat Millwall 3–0 in the final at the Millennium Stadium, Cardiff.

✂ 100 PLAYERS WHO SHOOK THE KOP ✂

In 2006 Liverpool produced a list entitled "100 Players who Shook the Kop". Over 100,000 fans of the Anfield club selected their personal Top Ten players in order of impact made and the results were collated to establish a Top 100. Five players who played for the club in the Premier League made the Top Ten (and a sixth, Michael Owen, was 14th):

1	Kenny Dalglish	1977–91
2	**Steven Gerrard**	1998–present
3	**Ian Rush**	1980–7 & 1988–96
4	**Robbie Fowler**	1993–2001 & 2006–07
5	**John Barnes**	1987–97
6	Billy Liddell	1938–1960
7	**Jamie Carragher**	1996–present
8	Kevin Keegan	1971–1977
9	Graeme Souness	1978–1984
10	Emlyn Hughes	1967–1979

MAN UTD PREMIER LEAGUE FANTASY XI

1
Edwin
VAN DER SAR

2
Gary
NEVILLE

6
Gary
PALLISTER

5
Rio
FERDINAND

3
Denis
IRWIN

4
Roy
KEANE
(capt.)

7
Eric
CANTONA

8
Paul
SCHOLES

9
Ruud van
NISTELROOY

10
Wayne
ROONEY

11
Ryan
GIGGS

Substitutes
Fabien *BARTHEZ* • Nemanja *VIDIC* • Steve *BRUCE* • Mark *HUGHES* •
David *BECKHAM* • Cristiano *RONALDO* • Robin *VAN PERSIE*

Manager
Sir Alex *FERGUSON* CBE

Did You Know That?
Sir Alex Ferguson managed the Scottish national team at the 1986
FIFA World Cup finals.

RELEGATED SIDE MAKE UEFA CUP

Despite finishing in 18th place in the Premiership table in season
2001–02, resulting in relegation to Division One, Ipswich Town
still qualified for the 2002–03 UEFA Cup qualifying round as Fair
Play Award winners.

UEFA CHAMPIONS LEAGUE 1-2-3

As well as the 1999–2000 Premiership champions Manchester
United and runners-up Arsenal, third-placed Leeds United also
qualified for the 2000–01 UEFA Champions League. Liverpool
finished fourth in the Premiership and had to settle for a UEFA
Cup berth, while FA Cup winners Chelsea and League Cup winners
Leicester City also gained UEFA Cup slots.

❧ FINAL PREMIERSHIP TABLE 1993–94 ❧

Pos Team	P	W	D	L	F	A	Pts
1. Manchester United (C)	42	27	11	4	80	38	92
2. Blackburn Rovers	42	25	9	8	63	36	84
3. Newcastle United	42	23	8	11	82	41	77
4. Arsenal	42	18	17	7	53	28	71
5. Leeds United	42	18	16	8	65	39	70
6. Wimbledon	42	18	11	13	56	53	65
7. Sheffield Wednesday	42	16	16	10	76	54	64
8. Liverpool FC	42	17	9	16	59	55	60
9. Queen's Park Rangers	42	16	12	14	62	61	60
10. Aston Villa	42	15	12	15	46	50	57
11. Coventry City	42	14	14	14	43	45	56
12. Norwich City	42	12	17	13	65	61	53
13. West Ham United	42	13	13	16	47	58	52
14. Chelsea	42	13	12	17	49	53	51
15. Tottenham Hotspur	42	11	12	19	54	59	45
16. Manchester City	42	9	18	15	38	49	45
17. Everton	42	12	8	22	42	63	44
18. Southampton	42	12	7	23	49	66	43
19. Ipswich Town	42	9	16	17	35	58	43
20. Sheffield United (R)	42	8	18	16	42	60	42
21. Oldham Athletic (R)	42	9	13	20	42	68	40
22. Swindon Town (R)	42	5	15	22	47	100	30

Did You Know That?

In season 1993–94 Tottenham Hotspur finished 15th in the Premiership table with 45 points, five places above the relegated teams. Exactly one year earlier in the inaugural Premiership season Crystal Palace were relegated after accumulating 49 points (Spurs finished in eighth place in 1992–93).

❧ CENTURION TROTTERS ❧

At the end of the 1996–97 season, Bolton Wanderers returned to the Premiership in majestic fashion after reaching 98 points and bagging an impressive 100 goals on the way to winning Division One. Barnsley joined the Trotters in English football's top flight thanks to their runners-up position, the first time they had reached such dizzy heights in the club's history. Crystal Palace ended their two-year sabbatical away from the big boys after clinching promotion to the Premiership via the play-offs.

❧ BLACK CATS SCREECH THE LOUDEST ❧

Prior to the Premiership games played over the weekend of 27–28 October 2007 a "Decibel Survey" was conducted by the telephone number service 118 118 to measure the noise factor at all 20 Premier League clubs' grounds. When the resulting "Crowd Noise Table" was published, Sunderland were top, the Black Cats' Stadium of Light measuring a deafening 129.2, while Fulham came bottom. Arsenal's Emirates Stadium, nicknamed "The Library", was 12th in the table.

❧ CHANGES DOWN BY THE RIVERSIDE ❧

At the end of the 2000–01 season Bryan Robson resigned as the manager of Middlesbrough after having spent seven years in charge of the club. The writing was on the wall for Robson during the season when Boro appointed the former England manager Terry Venables as his assistant. However, Venables also left at the end of the season after helping the club to the relative safe position of 14th in the table. Boro persuaded Sir Alex Ferguson's right-hand man, Steve McClaren, to take charge at The Riverside.

❧ SINGING THE BLUES ❧

When Chelsea beat Manchester United at Stamford Bridge on 29 April 2006, the result gave Jose Mourinho's men their second Premiership crown in a row. In the end the Blues retained their title by eight points from the eight-times Premiership champions Manchester United, with Liverpool one point further back in third place.

❧ ARSENE OF THE ARSENAL ❧

When Arsenal won the Premier League in season 1997–98, their French manager Arsene Wenger became the first foreign manager to win English football's top division.

❧ TOUGH FOR THE TYKES ❧

Season 1997–98 was Barnsley's first campaign in English football's top flight in the club's 102-year history. In spite of their shock defeat of Manchester United in the FA Cup they were out of their depth in the Premiership and hovered around the relegation zone all season long. They ended up making an immediate return to Division One and have not played Premiership football since.

⚜ THE BOY WONDER ⚜

On 19 October 2002, a spectacular last-minute strike from a 16-year-old named Wayne Rooney gave Everton a 2–1 win over Arsenal in the Premiership at Goodison Park. Rooney's goal against the England goalkeeper David Seaman ended the Gunners' impressive 30-game unbeaten run and propelled the kid from Croxteth on to the world stage. Rooney's wonder strike came five days before his 17th birthday and at the time made him the youngest-ever goalscorer in Premier League history. Rooney grew up supporting Everton, and Duncan Ferguson was his childhood hero. On one occasion after scoring a superb goal in the FA Youth Cup for Everton, Rooney lifted up his shirt to reveal a T-shirt underneath which read: "Once a blue, always a blue." However, the Goodison Park club could only hold on to the prodigious talent for two more seasons. After starring for England at the 2004 European Championships in Portugal he joined Manchester United.

⚜ IN THE BEGINNING ⚜

The following 22 teams resigned from the Football League to contest the new Premiership in the inaugural FA Premier League season of 1992–93:

❖ Arsenal ❖	❖ Manchester United ❖
❖ Aston Villa ❖	❖ Middlesbrough ❖
❖ Blackburn Rovers ❖	❖ Norwich City ❖
❖ Chelsea ❖	❖ Nottingham Forest ❖
❖ Coventry City ❖	❖ Oldham Athletic ❖
❖ Crystal Palace ❖	❖ Queen's Park Rangers ❖
❖ Everton ❖	❖ Sheffield United ❖
❖ Ipswich Town ❖	❖ Sheffield Wednesday ❖
❖ Leeds United ❖	❖ Southampton ❖
❖ Liverpool ❖	❖ Tottenham Hotspur ❖
❖ Manchester City ❖	❖ Wimbledon ❖

⚜ EUROPEAN TOFFEES ⚜

Everton beat Manchester United, Premiership runners-up in 1994–95 to Blackburn Rovers, 1–0 in the 1995 FA Cup final at Wembley. It meant that the Toffees, despite their lowly Premiership finish of 15th place, still managed to qualify for European football the following season, in the European Cup Winners' Cup, thanks to Paul Rideout's goal.

❧ RONNY'S QUINTUPLE DELIGHT ❧

In season 2006–07 Manchester United's Cristiano Ronaldo won five individual awards:

❖ PFA Players' Player of the Year ❖
❖ PFA Young Player of the Year ❖
❖ PFA Fans' Player of the Year ❖
❖ Football Writers' Association Footballer of the Year ❖
❖ Barclays Player of the Season ❖

Did you know that:
Just for good measure Cristiano Ronaldo was also named in the Premier League Team of the Year.

❧ FOLLOWING A LEGEND ❧

Manchester United spent a few short days in April 2013 doing something they had not done since November 1986: looking for a new manager. To follow in the giant footsteps of Sir Alex Ferguson, United chose another Scotsman, David Moyes, who had spent 11 years in charge at Everton. Sir Alex thought it was the right appointment as he said, "David is a man of great integrity with a strong work ethic. I've admired his work for a long time and approached him as far back as 1998 to discuss the position of assistant manager here. There is no question he has all the qualities we expect of a manager at this club."

Moyes said of his new challenge, "I am delighted that Sir Alex saw fit to recommend me for the job. I have great respect for everything he has done and for the football club. I know how hard it will be to follow the best manager ever, but the opportunity to manage Manchester United isn't something that comes around very often and I'm really looking forward to taking up the post next season."

❧ THE BOY WONDER ❧

On 24 February 2013, Swansea City beat League Two side Bradford City 5-0 at Wembley in the 2013 Capital One (League) Cup final to secure the club's first major trophy in their 101-year history. Bradford had knocked out three Premier League clubs to reach the final – Wigan Athletic, Arsenal and Aston Villa – and become the first side from English football's fourth tier to reach the final since 1962, when Rochdale lost 4–0 to Second Division Norwich City over two legs.

❧ PREMIER GROUNDS ❧

The following stadia have hosted Premier League football (1992–2013):

Arsenal	Highbury, Emirates Stadium
Aston Villa	Villa Park
Barnsley	Oakwell
Birmingham City	St Andrews
Blackburn Rovers	Ewood Park
Blackpool	Bloomfield Road
Bolton Wanderers	Burnden Park, Reebok Stadium
Bradford City	Valley Parade
Burnley	Turf Moor
Charlton Athletic	The Valley
Chelsea	Stamford Bridge
Coventry City	Highfield Road
Crystal Palace/Wimbledon	Selhurst Park
Derby County	Baseball Ground, Pride Park
Everton	Goodison Park
Fulham	Craven Cottage
Hull City	Kingston Communications Stadium
Ipswich Town	Portman Road
Leeds United	Elland Road
Leicester City	Filbert Street, Walkers Stadium
Liverpool	Anfield
Manchester City	Maine Road, City of Manchester Stadium (Eastlands, Etihad Stadium)
Manchester United	Old Trafford
Middlesbrough	Ayresome Park, Riverside Stadium
Newcastle United	St James' Park (Sports Direct Arena)
Norwich City	Carrow Road
Nottingham Forest	City Ground
Oldham Athletic	Boundary Park
Portsmouth	Fratton Park
Queen's Park Rangers	Loftus Road
Reading	Madejski Stadium
Sheffield United	Bramall Lane
Sheffield Wednesday	Hillsborough
Southampton	The Dell, St Mary's
Stoke City	Britannia Stadium
Sunderland	Roker Park, Stadium of Light
Swansea City	Britannia Stadium
Swindon Town	County Ground
Tottenham Hotspur	White Hart Lane
Watford	Vicarage Road
West Bromwich Albion	The Hawthorns
West Ham United	Upton Park
Wigan Athletic	JJB Stadium (DW Stadium)
Wolverhampton Wanderers	Molineux

Names in brackets are renamed Stadiums. Sports Direct Arena reverted after a few months.

❦ GERRARD TURNS 400 ❦

On 28 October 2007 Steven Gerrard appeared in his 400th game for Liverpool and scored in their 1–1 Premier League draw against Arsenal at Anfield. However, the Liverpool captain – who finished the 2012–13 seasons with 630 appearances – is some distance behind the club's record holder, Ian Callaghan, who played 848 games for the Reds over the course of 19 seasons from 1958 to 1978.

❦ NO NEW YEAR'S DAY CHEER ❦

For the first time in five years, New Year's Day 2009 saw no Premier League matches. This was because the FA Cup third round was played on the weekend of 3–4 January.

❦ THE WEST MIDLANDS FOUR ❦

For the first time in 27 seasons, four West Midlands clubs played in the Premier League in 2010–11: Aston Villa, Birmingham City, West Bromwich Albion and Wolverhampton Wanderers. It didn't last because Birmingham were relegated at the end of the season. Albion's two Derbies against Wolves were the first in the Premier League era.

❦ A HAT-TRICK OF DEPARTURES ❦

At the end of the 1997–98 season Everton narrowly avoided relegation from the Premier Ldeague, finishing one place above the drop zone on goal difference. In spite of having helped Everton preserve their status in English football's top flight for the 45th consecutive season, Howard Kendall resigned as manager. It was the third time the former Everton player had vacated the manager's job at Goodison Park. Walter Smith, the manager of Glasgow Rangers, replaced Kendall.

❦ EIGHT FROM 11 FOR RED DEVILS ❦

The 2002–03 season was the 11th season of the Premier League, and it was won by Manchester United – their eighth Premiership title. In the final two months of the season Manchester United were simply awesome as they managed to overhaul an eight-point advantage held by the defending champions Arsenal at the beginning of March. Arsenal limped out of the title race in the penultimate game of the season, losing at home to relegation-threatened Leeds United. Once again the Premier League was sponsored by Barclaycard.

☙ PREMIERSHIP TALK (3) ❧

"I gave an interview to Radio 4 about the vocabulary of English football and how you quickly become familiar with it."
David Ginola (Aston Villa)

☙ THE ELITE EIGHT ❧

Only eight English sides have never been outside the top two divisions: Arsenal, Chelsea, Everton, Liverpool, Manchester United, Newcastle United, Tottenham Hotspur and West Ham United. Leeds United and Leicester City were members of this exclusive club until they were relegated to League One (the old Third Division) at the end of the 2006–07 and 2007–08 seasons, respectively.

☙ FIVE IN A ROW FOR FERGIE ❧

When Manchester United won the Premier League and FA Cup double in 1993–94, it was the fifth successive year in which Alex Ferguson had guided the club to silverware success:

1990	FA Cup
1991	European Cup Winners' Cup & European Super Cup
1992	League Cup
1993	FA Premier League
1994	FA Premier League & FA Cup

Did You Know That:
Not surprisingly Fergie was named the Premier League Manager of the Year for 1992–93.

☙ A MYSTERY ILLNESS ❧

Going into the final game of the 2005–06 season Spurs sat fourth in the Premiership table, the last UEFA Champions League qualifying spot, with Arsenal one place below them. All Spurs had to do was achieve a better result away to West Ham United than Arsenal, who were at home to Wigan Athletic. However, the night before the match a number of the Spurs players fell ill. Spurs approached the FA seeking to delay the kick-off, but the FA refused. West Ham United won the game 2–1, while Arsenal beat Wigan 4–1 to secure the last UEFA Champions League qualification slot and Spurs had to settle for a place in the UEFA Cup.

❧ TRACTOR BOY CAUSES BIG SURPRISE ❧

At newly promoted Ipswich Town striker Marcus Stewart was the unknown quantity at the start of the 2000–01 season. However, Stewart's 19 Premier League goals helped his side to fifth in the table and he finished runner-up to Chelsea's prolific frontman Jimmy Floyd Hasselbaink in the Premier League goalscoring table.

❧ THE TRIO TO BEAT THE DOUBLE WINNERS ❧

During their Double-winning season of 2001–02 Arsenal only suffered three defeats – at the hands of Charlton Athletic, Leeds United and Newcastle United and all, ironically, at home.

❧ LIGHTWEIGHT BANTAMS ❧

In November 2000 Bradford City dismissed Chris Hutchings after just six months in charge of the Bantams and 12 Premiership games and replaced him with Jim Jeffries from Hearts. However, Jeffries could not save the Yorkshire club from relegation, and they dropped into Division One after just two seasons in the Premiership, having finished bottom of the table. They have not returned since.

❧ KEEGAN QUITS GEORDIES ❧

On 5 January 1997, Kevin Keegan sent shockwaves around Newcastle after deciding it was time he quit his position as manager. Keegan took over at St James' Park in February 1992 when the Geordies lay second from bottom of the old Second Division. However, Super Kev helped save Newcastle United from relegation and the following season (1992–93) the Magpies won the new First Division Championship title and were promoted to the Premier League. In their first season in the Premiership they finished third in the table followed by a sixth-place finish in 1994–95. The following season Keegan steered Newcastle to the brink of the Premier League title, only for his team to fall away towards the end of the season and finish runners-up to Manchester United. When he walked out of St James' Park, Newcastle were well placed in the Premiership, and they ended the season runners-up to Manchester United once again, but Keegan said that he was quitting because he felt he had taken the club as far as he could. Newcastle United moved swiftly and replaced Keegan with Kenny Dalglish, who had guided Blackburn Rovers to Premiership success in 1994–95.

⚡ ERIC CANTONA ⚡

Eric Daniel Pierre Cantona was born in Paris on 24 May 1966. When he was sensationally transferred from Leeds United to Manchester United in November 1992, some Manchester United fans questioned the signing. Over the following five seasons United won four Premier League titles, two FA Cups and two Doubles. Eric almost single-handedly rewrote the history books of Manchester United.

Prior to arriving at Old Trafford, Eric had played for Auxerre, Montpellier, Nantes and Leeds United. Sheffield Wednesday passed up on the opportunity to sign him when he was on trial with them in 1991, but the Owls' loss was Leeds United's gain when Howard Wilkinson teamed him up with Gordon Strachan and the pair helped Leeds win the last ever First Division title in 1991–92. Strangely, it was a telephone call from Wilkinson to Alex Ferguson that led to Eric joining the Red Devils. The Leeds manager wanted to find out whether Denis Irwin was for sale. Ferguson said he was not, then cheekily asked about Eric's availability. Within days the Frenchman joined Manchester United for a bargain fee of £1 million. On 6 December 1992, Eric made his debut as a substitute for Manchester United in a 2–1 home win over Manchester City. The Frenchman's arrival completely transformed United's performances on the pitch with his skill, his composure, his creativity and his goals.

On a number of occasions Eric's fiery temper got him into trouble both on and off the pitch. In December 1991, he was suspended for calling each member of a French disciplinary committee an idiot at a hearing. And, in January 1995, Eric famously exacted his own revenge on a Crystal Palace fan who verbally abused him as he walked off the pitch following a red card at Selhurst Park – Eric's kung fu moment.

However, Eric will always be remembered for his genius on the pitch, his aura of invincibility, his Gallic flair, his grace and composure, his amazing goals and, not least, his famous turned-up collar. United fans affectionately dubbed him "The King". He once said of Manchester United: "I am in love with Manchester United. It is like finding a wife who has given me the perfect marriage." In 1998, the Football League, as part of its centenary season celebrations, included Eric in its list of 100 League Legends, and in 2002 his remarkable achievements in English football were recognized when he was made an inaugural inductee of the English Football Hall of Fame.

Did you know that:
Despite his success with United, Eric Cantona did not play international football after France failed to qualify for the 1994 World Cup finals.

❧ BOSS FOR AN AFTERNOON ❧

Clive Allen took temporary charge of Tottenham Hotspur for their home Premiership game against Blackburn Rovers at White Hart Lane on 27 October 2007 while the newly appointed manager, Juande Ramos, sat in the stands with Daniel Levy, the club's chairman. Spurs lost 2–1, and Allen's tenure was the shortest in Premiership history: it lasted just a single afternoon, as Ramos took over the reins straight after the game ended.

❧ SIR LES' SIX-PACK ❧

The much-travelled Les Ferdinand scored just one Premier League goal for Bolton Wanderers in the 2004–05 season. However, it proved to be a landmark goal for "Sir Les", making him the first player to score in the Premiership for six different clubs: Queen's Park Rangers, Newcastle United, Tottenham Hotspur, West Ham United, Leicester City and Bolton Wanderers. Two years later, in 2006–07, Andy Cole (Newcastle United, Manchester United, Fulham, Blackburn Rovers, Manchester City and Portsmouth) equalled his achievement. Five more players have since emulated Ferdinand and Cole.

Player	Clubs
Marcus Bent	Charlton Athletic, Everton, Ipswich Town Leicester City, Crystal Palace, Wigan Athletic
Nick Barmby	Tottenham Hotspur, Middlesbrough Everton, Liverpool, Leeds United, Hull City
Craig Bellamy	Coventry City, Newcastle United, Liverpool, Blackburn Rovers, West Ham United, Manchester City
Robbie Keane	Aston Villa, Coventry City, Liverpool Tottenham Hotspur, Leeds United West Ham United
Peter Crouch	Aston Villa, Southampton, Liverpool, Portsmouth, Tottenham Hotspur, Stoke City

❧ POOR TRAVELLERS ❧

During the 1999–2000 season Coventry City played 19 Premier League away games without recording a single victory on their travels (W 0, D 7, L 12, For 9, Against 32). Amazingly, the Sky Blues still managed to finish 14th in the Premiership table thanks to 12 home wins and one home draw at Highfield Road.

⚜ FINAL PREMIERSHIP TABLE 1994–95 ⚜

Pos	Team	P	W	D	L	F	A	Pts
1	Blackburn Rovers (C)	42	27	8	7	80	39	89
2	Manchester United	42	26	10	6	77	28	88
3	Nottingham Forest	42	22	11	9	72	43	77
4	Liverpool	42	21	11	10	65	37	74
5	Leeds United	42	20	13	9	59	38	73
6	Newcastle United	42	20	12	10	67	47	72
7	Tottenham Hotspur	42	16	14	12	66	58	62
8	Queen's Park Rangers	42	17	9	16	61	59	60
9	Wimbledon	42	15	11	16	48	65	56
10	Southampton	42	12	18	12	61	63	54
11	Chelsea	42	13	15	14	50	55	54
12	Arsenal	42	13	12	17	52	49	51
13	Sheffield Wednesday	42	13	12	17	49	57	51
14	West Ham United	42	13	11	18	44	48	50
15	Everton	42	11	17	14	44	51	50
16	Coventry City	42	12	14	16	44	62	50
17	Manchester City	42	12	13	17	53	64	49
18	Aston Villa	42	11	15	16	51	56	48
19	Crystal Palace (R)	42	11	12	19	34	49	45
20	Norwich City (R)	42	10	13	19	37	54	43
21	Leicester City (R)	42	6	11	25	45	80	29
22	Ipswich Town (R)	42	7	6	29	36	93	27

⚜ TOP FLIGHT RECORDS ⚜

Season 2012–13 was Arsenal's 92th consecutive appearance in the top flight of English football (1920–present) while Everton hold the record for spending the most seasons in the top flight, 112 (1888–1930 & 1954–present).

⚜ FERGIE'S FLEDGELINGS ⚜

At the end of 1994–95, three players who had helped Manchester United win the Premiership title in 1992–93 and the Double in 1993–94 all left Old Trafford. Mark Hughes joined Chelsea, Paul Ince moved to Inter Milan and Everton made United's "Flying Russian", Andrei Kanchelskis, their new club record signing at £5 million. Many viewed the influential trio's departure as the start of the Red Devils' demise, but it actually marked the onset of one of the most successful periods in the club's history, the beginning of Fergie's Fledgelings.

❧ TREBLE WINNERS ❧

The 1998–99 season will always be remembered for the fact that Manchester United won an unprecedented treble of Premier League, FA Cup and UEFA Champions League. United and Arsenal went head to head all season long with the Gunners beating the Red Devils twice early in the season (3–0 in the Community Shield at Wembley and 3–0 in the Premiership at Highbury). However, when the season ended, United had beaten the 1997–98 Double winners to the Premiership crown by a single point thanks to a dramatic 2–1 win over Tottenham Hotspur at Old Trafford on the final day; had beaten Newcastle United 2–0 in the FA Cup final at Wembley after knocking the Gunners out in a replay in the semi-final in one of the most exciting FA Cup games ever played; and had won the UEFA Champions League in Barcelona's Camp Nou stadium after scoring two goals in injury time to beat Bayern Munich 2–1. Their UEFA Champions League victory came on what would have been Sir Matt Busby's 90th birthday, 26 May 1999.

❧ FRENCH BRIGADE BEGINS AT ARSENAL ❧

Six weeks into the 1996–97 season, Arsenal appointed 46-year-old Frenchman Arsene Wenger as their new manager. Wenger had been working in Japan, having previously managed AS Monaco.

❧ MAKE IT A DOUBLE DOUBLE ❧

In season 1995–96, Manchester United completed a remarkable second domestic Double, the first club to achieve this. First of all United reined in Newcastle United's 12-point lead in the Premiership, with the crunch fixture of the season coming at St James' Park on 4 March 1996. United went into the game trailing the Geordies by four points, but a goal from the enigmatic Eric Cantona gave the Red Devils a 1–0 win over the Geordies and provided the momentum they needed to win their third Premiership crown in four years, a truly remarkable achievement. And it was the French genius who gave United the double Double when he scored the only goal of the game to beat Liverpool 1–0 at Wembley in the 1996 FA Cup final.

❧ RUSH TRANSFER ❧

On 1 June 1996, Ian Rush left Liverpool (for a second time) and joined Leeds United on a free transfer.

♘ TAKING THE BULL BY THE HORNS ♞

When Juande Ramos took charge of Tottenham Hotspur in late October 2007, he brought with him to White Hart Lane his tough fitness trainer from Seville, Marcos Alvarez. The 36-year-old Alvarez is a former professional tennis player and the personal fitness trainer to the bullfighter Fran Rivera. Alvarez is renowned as a hard taskmaster on the training pitch, and on one occasion in his early days at Seville several of the players drew a joke picture of Alvarez with paper stuffed in his mouth so he couldn't instruct them to do any more running. However, the Seville players' fitness paid off when they won the UEFA Cup in 2005–06, the UEFA Super Cup in 2005–06, the Copa del Rey (Spanish Cup) and Spanish Super Cup in 2006–07 and the UEFA Cup again in 2006–07.

♘ INAUGURAL PFA TEAM OF THE YEAR ♞

The inaugural PFA Team of the Year was selected following the 2002–03 season and was made up as follows:

1. Brad Friedel.............................Blackburn Rovers
2. Stephen Carr............................Tottenham Hotspur
3. Ashley Cole..............................Arsenal
4. Patrick Vieira...........................Arsenal
5. Sol Campbell............................Arsenal
6. William Gallas..........................Chelsea
7. Robert Pires.............................Arsenal
8. Paul Scholes.............................Manchester United
9. Alan Shearer............................Newcastle United
10. Thierry Henry..........................Arsenal
11. Kieron Dyer............................Newcastle United

♘ A TRIO OF RELEGATED CITIES ♞

When Derby County beat Manchester United 1–0 at Old Trafford on 5 May 2001 the result meant that Coventry City were relegated after 34 years in the top flight. Derby County ended the season in 17th place in the table, just one place above Manchester City, who along with bottom-of-the-table Bradford City also went down into Division One. Many Coventry and Manchester City fans questioned the Rams' victory, claiming that United, already assured of the championship, simply did not try – in order to ensure that local rivals Manchester City went down.

✂ YOU'LL NEVER WALK ALONE ✂

The song "You'll Never Walk Alone" was written by Richard Rodgers and Oscar Hammerstein II for their 1945 musical Carousel. The first occasion when the song was sung at a football match was in 1958 at Old Trafford, the home of Manchester United. At the time the New Mills Operatic Society was rehearsing for their performance of Carousel, and they sang the song at a Manchester United home game to honour the 23 people (including eight Manchester United players) who tragically lost their lives in the Munich air disaster on 6 February 1958. At subsequent United home games the fans sang the song, and they continued to do so until 1963 when the Liverpool band Gerry and the Pacemakers recorded it and released it as a single. The United faithful quickly dropped the song from their Old Trafford match-day repertoire. On 4 November 1963, it reached No. 1 in the pop charts and stayed there for four weeks before being ousted by the Beatles' "I Want to Hold Your Hand". The Liverpool fans then adopted it as the club's anthem, and it is traditionally sung before the start and at the end of all their home games at Anfield. Even Elvis Presley recorded the song, but he only just managed to squeeze into the Top 100 with his version in 1968. In July 1998 Jose Carreras, Placido Domingo and Luciano Pavarotti released an operatic version of the song which reached No. 21 in the UK music charts.

✂ MONEY FOR ACORNS ✂

When Aston Villa's Marc Albrighton equalised against Arsenal at Villa Park on 21 December 2011, he scored the 20,000th goal in Premiership history (the Gunners went on to win 2–1). League sponsors Barclays gave him £20,000 by to donate to a charity of his choice and he chose the Birmingham-based Acorns Children's Hospice. In 2009–10 Villa had Acorns on their shirts.

✂ THE NOT SO MAGNIFICENT SEVEN ✂

From 2008, the FA let Premier League clubs name seven substitutes on their team-sheets, but, as before, only three could be used.

✂ LIVERPOOL EMPLOY A DIGGER ✂

John Barnes' nickname at Liverpool was "Digger" – not to imply that his displays in the heart of midfield were merely workmanlike, but because his initials are "JCB" – John Charles Barnes.

❧ ARSENAL PREMIER LEAGUE FANTASY XI ❧

1
David
SEAMAN

2
Lee
DIXON

5
Sol
CAMPBELL

6
Tony
ADAMS
(Capt.)

3
Nigel
WINTERBURN

7
Robert
PIRES

4
Patrick
VIEIRA

8
Dennis
BERGKAMP

9
Ian
WRIGHT

10
Thierry
HENRY

11
Robin
VAN PERSIE

Substitutes
Jens *LEHMANN* • Ashley *COLE* • Martin *KEOWN* •
Emmanuel *PETIT* • Nicolas *ANELKA* • Theo *WALCOTT* • Jack *WILSHERE*

Manager
Arsene *WENGER* OBE

Did You Know That?
Of the British clubs, only Liverpool (16) have played in more
European finals than Arsenal (7).

❧ GEORDIES ON THE SLIDE ❧

Newcastle United finished runners-up in the Premiership in 1995–96
and 1996–97 under Kevin Keegan, but Kenny Dalglish could only
guide the Geordies to 13th place in 1997–98, his first full season in
charge at St James' Park. The main problem was that Alan Shearer
suffered a serious ankle injury before the season and was out of action
until February 1998. Another reason was that both Les Ferdinand and
David Ginola were sold to Tottenham Hotspur, and their replacements,
John Barnes and Ian Rush, failed to make the grade. However, despite
a miserable Premiership campaign, Newcastle made it all the way to
Wembley for the FA Cup final, their first since 1974, but they lost
2–0 to Arsenal. Despite losing the final, the Magpies still achieved a
place in Europe for 1998–99, in the European Cup Winners' Cup, on
account of Arsenal's league and cup Double.

❧ PREMIERSHIP TALK (4) ❧

"If I'd had a gun, I would've shot him."
Aston Villa manager **John Gregory** *after Dwight Yorke signed for Manchester United in 1998*

❧ MEGA BUCKS ❧

During the 2007–08 season, Premiership salaries and bonuses exceeded the £1 billion barrier for the first time in the Premier League's history, helped by the new £1.7 billion television deal for top-flight games coming into effect.

❧ ST PATRICK'S DAY LUCK ❧

On 17 March 2007, Paul Robinson of Tottenham Hotspur and England scored a goal against his opposite number from an 83-yard free-kick. The ball bounced over Watford's on-loan goalkeeper Ben Foster in Spurs' 3–1 win at White Hart Lane. In the 15-year history of the FA Premier League it was only the third time a goalkeeper had scored in a game. The other two goals were scored by Aston Villa's Peter Schmeichel, against Everton on 21 October 2001 (Schmeichel also scored in the UEFA Cup for Manchester United), and Brad Friedel, playing for Blackburn Rovers against Charlton Athletic on 21 February 2004. However, Robinson was the only goalkeeper to score for the winning team.

❧ CRAZY GANG LOSE RELEGATION FIGHT ❧

Wimbledon manager Egil Olsen, appointed prior to the start of the 1999–2000 season, was sacked two games before it ended, being replaced by coach Terry Burton. Olsen had led the Norwegian national side to successive FIFA World Cup finals tournaments in 1994 and 1998, but failed to impress in the Premiership. On the last day of the 1999–2000 season Wimbledon lay one place above the relegation zone on goal difference. However, a 3–0 defeat to Southampton at The Dell, combined with Bradford City's surprise 1–0 home win over Liverpool, brought the Crazy Gang's 14-year tenure in the top flight to an end. It was a sad end for the team who had enjoyed a fairytale existence in the Premiership, having only been elected to the Football League in 1977, winning promotion to the top Division in 1986 and achieving a shock 1–0 win over Liverpool in the 1988 FA Cup final at Wembley.

♔ GALLAS HAT-TRICK ♕

Arsenal drew 2–2 with Manchester United at Emirates Stadium in a top of the table Premiership encounter on 3 November 2007. Gallas turned the ball into his own net to give United a 1–0 lead at the interval before Cesc Fabregas scored his 11th goal of the season to level the game early in the second half. A goal from Cristiano Ronaldo looked set to give the reigning champions all three points before Gallas scored late in the game. It was the French defender's third goal against United and for a third different team (the others having been scored for Olympique Marseille and Chelsea).

♔ NOT AN ENGLISHMAN IN SIGHT ♕

In season 2000–01 not one of the top six teams in the Premier League at the end of the season had an English manager:

1. Manchester United......Sir Alex Ferguson...............Scottish
2. Arsenal...........................Arsene Wenger.......................French
3. Liverpool.........................Gerard Houllier.....................French
4. Leeds United.................David O'Leary..........................Irish
5. Ipswich Town................George Burley........................Scottish
6. Chelsea...........................Claudio Ranieri......................Italian

Did You Know That:
Peter Reid, a former England international, guided Sunderland to seventh place.

♔ LOTS OF POMP ♕

Harry Redknapp left Portsmouth in November 2004, becoming boss at Southampton. He was replaced by Pompey executive director Velimir Zajec, but Alain Perrin succeeded him four months later. Harry went back to Portsmouth in late 2005 and won the FA Cup there in 2008.

♔ IDLE BOAST ♕

After three games of the 2001–02 season an unfamiliar name headed the Premier League table, Bolton Wanderers. The Trotters had won their opening three games to lead the field, and their manager Sam Allardyce made the bold claim that his side could win the club's first ever championship title. When the season ended, Bolton Wanderers lay 16th in the table, two places above the relegation zone.

❧ FIRST PREMIER LEAGUE CHAMPIONS ❧

The first-ever FA Premier League championship title in season 1992–93 was won by Manchester United, their first top-flight crown in 26 years (since 1966–67). Aston Villa, managed by Ron Atkinson, finished runners-up ten points adrift of the champions. United, managed by Alex Ferguson, had chased Villa for most of the season, while Norwich City were also in the hunt for the prestige of being crowned the Premier League's inaugural champions. Amazingly, Norwich City, managed by Mike Walker, led the Premiership at Christmas with a negative goals difference and finished the season in a highly respectable third place to guarantee themselves UEFA Cup football the following season. Newly promoted Blackburn Rovers surpassed all expectations by finishing in fourth place. Spearheaded by their new £3.6m acquisition from Southampton, Alan Shearer, they played an entertaining attacking brand of football and gave Norwich City a 7–1 thumping. Nottingham Forest, European Cup winners in 1979 and 1980, had a dismal season and were rooted to the foot of the table for the vast part of the campaign. Even before Forest were relegated their legendary manager, the outspoken yet colourful Brian Clough, took the decision to retire from football after 28 years in various hot seats across England (Hartlepool United 1965–67, Derby County 1967–73, Brighton & Hove Albion 1973–74, Leeds United 1974 & Nottingham Forest 1975–93). Newly promoted Middlesbrough followed Forest and dropped out of the top flight along with Crystal Palace. Oldham produced a dramatic 4–3 win over Southampton at The Dell on the last day of the season to stay up on goal difference ahead of Palace, who would have stayed up and sent Oldham Athletic down if they had won their final league game. Like Clough, Palace manager Steve Coppell tendered his resignation. Clough was replaced by former Forest player Frank Clark, while Palace appointed Alan Smith as Coppell's successor.

❧ FIFA REJECT CLUBS' 39TH STEP ❧

On 14 March 2008, FIFA's executive committee unanimously opposed the Premier League's plan to play a 39th game of the season overseas. Two months earlier the Premier League unveiled its plan to host a 39th round of matches spread across five cities across the world from season 2011–12. "This idea to play a 39th round outside the country does not work. Even the former chairman of the FA, Mr Geoff Thompson, said we should oppose it," said Sepp Blatter the president of FIFA.

❧ FROM DEVILS TO SAINTS ❧

Club	Nickname
Arsenal	The Gunners
Aston Villa	The Villains
Barnsley	The Tykes
Birmingham City	The Blues
Blackpool	The Tangerines or The Seasiders
Blackburn Rovers	Rovers
Bolton Wanderers	The Trotters
Bradford City	The Bantams
Burnley	The Clarets
Charlton Athletic	The Addicks
Chelsea	The Blues
Coventry City	The Sky Blues
Crystal Palace	The Eagles
Derby County	The Rams
Everton	The Toffees
Fulham	The Cottagers
Hull City	The Tigers
Ipswich Town	The Tractor Boys
Leeds United	United
Leicester City	The Foxes
Liverpool	The Reds
Manchester City	The Blues
Manchester United	The Red Devils
Middlesbrough	Boro
Newcastle United	The Magpies
Norwich City	The Canaries
Nottingham Forest	The Reds
Oldham Athletic	The Latics
Portsmouth	Pompey
Queen's Park Rangers	The "R's"
Reading	The Royals
Sheffield United	The Blades
Sheffield Wednesday	The Owls
Southampton	The Saints
Stoke City	The Potters
Sunderland	The Black Cats
Swanssea City	The Swans
Swindon Town	The Robins
Tottenham Hotspur	Spurs
Watford	The Hornets
West Bromwich Albion	The Baggies
West Ham United	The Hammers
Wigan Athletic	The Latics
Wimbledon	The Dons
Wolverhampton Wanderers	Wolves

✌ UNITED WIN LEAGUE TREBLE ✌

Manchester United won the 2000–01 Premier League Championship title, their third in succession, and it was the dominant Red Devils' seventh Premiership from the nine contested (their 14th title in total). And for the third consecutive year it was Arsenal who ended up in runners-up spot. Sir Alex Ferguson became the first manager in English football history to win three championships in a row, although Huddersfield Town (1923–24, 1924–25 & 1925–26), Arsenal (1931–32, 1932–33 & 1933–34) and Liverpool (1981–82, 1982–83 & 1983–84) all managed three consecutive First Division championship wins in their history.

✌ A RUUD AFFAIR ✌

Ruud Gullit, Chelsea's player-manager, helped the Blues to FA Cup glory in his first season in charge at Stamford Bridge. Chelsea's 1997 FA Cup win over Middlesbrough at Wembley not only ended the club's 26-year spell without a major trophy, but also made Gullit the first foreign manager to win a major trophy with an English club.

✌ STRIKER SCORES WITH PAGE 3 PIN-UP ✌

In 1996 the Wimbledon striker Dean Holdsworth was involved in a highly publicized tabloid scandal when it was revealed he was having an extra-marital affair with Linsey Dawn McKenzie, a Page Three model with the *Sun* newspaper.

✌ SCOTS ON TOP ✌

Two Scotsmen won the end-of-season managerial awards in 2008–09. Everton boss David Moyes was the League Managers' Association Manager of the Year for achieving a second straight fifth-place finish for the Toffees – they were also runners-up in the FA Cup, losing 2–1 to Chelsea. Sir Alex Ferguson won his ninth Barclays Manager of the Season award in after guiding Manchester United to an 11th Premier League title

✌ TINY TOES ✌

Jose Dominguez of Tottenham Hotspur (1997–2000) is the smallest player ever to play in the Premier League, he stood only 5 feet 2 inches high.

♘ FINAL PREMIERSHIP TABLE 1995–96 ♘

Pos Team	P	W	D	L	F	A	Pts
1. Manchester United (C)	38	25	7	6	73	35	82
2. Newcastle United	38	24	6	8	66	37	78
3. Liverpool	38	20	11	7	70	34	71
4. Aston Villa	38	18	9	11	52	35	63
5. Arsenal	38	17	12	9	49	32	63
6. Everton	38	17	10	11	64	44	61
7. Blackburn Rovers	38	18	7	13	61	47	61
8. Tottenham Hotspur	38	16	13	9	50	38	61
9. Nottingham Forest	38	15	13	10	50	54	58
10. West Ham United	38	14	9	15	43	52	51
11. Chelsea	38	12	14	12	46	44	50
12. Middlesbrough	38	11	10	17	35	50	43
13. Leeds United	38	12	7	19	40	57	43
14. Wimbledon	38	10	11	17	55	70	41
15. Sheffield Wednesday	38	10	10	18	48	61	40
16. Coventry City	38	8	14	16	42	60	38
17. Southampton	38	9	11	18	34	52	38
18. Manchester City (R)	38	9	11	18	33	58	38
19. Queen's Park Rangers (R)	38	9	6	23	38	57	33
20. Bolton Wanderers (R)	38	8	5	25	39	71	29

♘ GUNNERS UNLUCKY 13 ♘

Arsenal's 2–2 home draw with Manchester United on 3 November 2007 was the first game the Gunners had failed to win in London in season 2007–08 in 13 games played – ten in the Premier League (three away), two in the UEFA Champions League and one in the Carling Cup.

♘ TRIPLE HAT-TRICK KINGS ♘

Only three players have scored a hat-trick in the Premier League for three different clubs:

Kevin Campbell – *Arsenal, Nottingham Forest, Everton*
Les Ferdinand – *Queen's Park Rangers, Newcastle United, Tottenham Hotspur*
Teddy Sheringham – *Tottenham Hotspur, Manchester United, Portsmouth*

♫ PREMIERSHIP TALK (5) ♫

"Please don't call me arrogant because what I'm saying is true. I'm
European champion, so I'm not one of the bottle. I think I'm a
special one... We have top players and, sorry if I'm arrogant, we have
a top manager."
Chelsea manager Jose Mourinho, 2004

♫ UNITED'S ALL-TIME TOP TEN ♫

On 19 February 2001, Manchester United's official club magazine
celebrated the publication of its 100th edition by publishing an
all-time Top 100 of Manchester United players based on a fans'
poll conducted by the magazine. Eric Cantona was the fans' No. 1
choice, with the legendary George Best in second place. In addition
to United's talismanic French maestro, Cantona, five other players
who played for United in the Premier League featured in the Top
Ten (indicated in the table with an *). When George Best was asked
for his comments on the fans' vote in an interview with the magazine
he said: "This side has done the Treble, which many people said
would never be done. I mean, winning the Double was considered
almost impossible at one time – and they did that twice. But it's a
bit unfair to compare eras."

Manchester United All-time Top Ten Players

1: Eric Cantona*	6: Bryan Robson*
2: George Best	7: Roy Keane*
3: Ryan Giggs*	8: David Beckham*
4: Bobby Charlton	9: Duncan Edwards
5: Peter Schmeichel*	10: Denis Law

♫ COVENTRY TOP DOGS ♫

Coventry City were the first ever leaders of the FA Premier League as
the 1992–93 season got under way. Their striker Mick Quinn scored
10 Premier League goals in their first six Premiership games.

♫ BLACK CATS PUNCH ABOVE THEIR WEIGHT ♫

In season 1999–2000 Sunderland's Kevin Phillips scored 30 Premier
League goals, making him the Premiership's top goalscorer for the
season. His goals helped the newly promoted Black Cats finish in a
highly respectable seventh place in the Premiership table.

❦ UNITED IN A CLASS OF THEIR OWN ❦

Manchester United lead the way in the Premier League's all-time goalscoring charts. The 13-time champions have found the back of opponents' nets 1,627 times, the only club to pass the 1,500 mark. In fact, over the 21 seasons of the competition, Arsenal – second in the table – average 10 goals per season fewer than United.

❦ JINXED PLAYERS ❦

In the Premier League's 21 seasons up to 2012–13, four players have been relegated with four different Premiership clubs:

Player	Clubs and years
Ashley Ward	Norwich City 1995, Barnsley 1998, Blackburn Rovers 1999, Bradford City 2001
Nathan Blake	Sheffield United 1994, Bolton Wanderers 1996/1998, Blackburn Rovers 1999, Wolverhampton Wanderers 2004
Nigel Quashie	Queen's Park Rangers 1996, Nottingham Forest 1999, Southampton 2005, West Bromwich Albion 2006
Herman Hreidarsson	Crystal Palace 1998, Wimbledon 2000, Ipswich Town 2002, Charlton Athletic 2007

❦ BRILLIANT BECKS ❦

Manchester United midfielder David Beckham won the 1996–97 PFA Young Player of the Year Award and a second Premiership winners' medal, his superb form having helped the Red Devils retain the title.

❦ IT'S A YOUNG MAN'S GAME ❦

Aston Villa's Ashley Young won the PFA Young Player of the Year award in 2008–09.

❦ A PAIR OF RUUD AWARDS ❦

Ruud van Nistelrooy won the Barclaycard Player of the Year Award for 2002–03 after helping Manchester United win their eighth Premiership title. The Dutch international also picked up the coveted Barclaycard Golden Boot Award after firing in 25 goals in his 38 Premiership games (equalling his own record of eight goals in eight successive Premiership games), and a massive 44 in all competitions for the champions.

❧ THE ENVY OF MILLIONS ❧

Upon taking up his post as manager of Manchester City at the start of the 1995–96 season, Alan Ball said that his job was "the envy of millions". However, the Blues failed to record a win in their opening 12 Premiership games, and a 2–2 draw at Maine Road on the final day of the season saw them relegated. City ended the campaign on 38 points, the same number as Coventry City and Southampton, but Manchester City went down because they had the worst goal difference of the trio. Sadly Alan died in 2007.

❧ BLUES BRING REDS DOWN TO EARTH ❧

Manchester United lost their first Premiership home game in over two years on 2 November 1996, losing 2–1 to Chelsea at Old Trafford.

❧ FAIR PLAY CITY ❧

Although Manchester City finished the 2002–03 season down in ninth place, three places below the automatic UEFA Cup qualifying slots, they qualified for the UEFA Cup for season 2003–04 – their first season in Europe in a quarter of a century – via the "fair play ranking".

❧ ARSENAL'S THIRD DOUBLE ❧

In season 2001–02 Arsenal, runners-up to Manchester United in the three previous Premiership campaigns, finally got the better of the men from Old Trafford. Arsenal, United and Liverpool were involved in a season-long battle for the title, but it was the Gunners' end-of-season form that ensured the Premier League trophy would be sitting in the Highbury boardroom for the first time in four years. The Gunners won their last 13 Premiership games and clinched the title at Old Trafford on 8 May 2002 thanks to Sylvain Wiltord's strike in a 1–0 win over the reigning champions. Arsenal were crowned champions for the 12th time in their history, winning their second Premiership crown and finishing seven points ahead of Liverpool and ten ahead of United. Arsenal then beat Chelsea 2–0 in the 2002 FA Cup final at the Millennium Stadium, Cardiff, to secure their third domestic Double, equalling a feat previously achieved only by Manchester United. Arsenal's Double-winning seasons were 1970–71, 1997–98 and 2001–02, whereas United won all of their Doubles during the 1990s (1993–94, 1995–96 and 1998–99).

♘ SIR ALEX FERGUSON CBE ♞

Sir Alex Ferguson has won more trophies than any other manager in the history of English football and has been in charge of Manchester United for more than 1,000 matches. He is Manchester United's longest-serving manager for with 26 years under his belt. The man Reds fans simply call "The Boss" has transformed the Old Trafford club into one of the biggest, richest and most feared clubs in the world. A master motivator of his players, he is also a genius at mind games with other managers, as Kevin Keegan, Arsene Wenger and Jose Mourinho among others will all attest. Things were nearly very different on two occasions. First, in 1989–90, there were rumblings that United had to win something that season or Ferguson might be shown the door. Lee Martin's 1990 FA Cup Final replay goal was enough to bring silverware to Old Trafford.

United's domination of the Premier League under Ferguson is phenomenal. Thirteen titles in 21 seasons and a worst finish of third is unlikely ever to be matched. This excludes knock-out competiton glory, domestic and European, which has seen United celebrate success in all bar the UEFA Cup/UEFA Europa League.

The greatest night of Ferguson's United career came in 1999, when United scored twice in the final seconds to snatch the UEFA Champions League from Bayern Munich in Barcelona. United thus completed a unique treble of Championship, FA Cup and Champions League, to go with League and FA Cup doubles achieved in 1994 and 1996.

Alex Ferguson received a knighthood for services to football following the 1999 Champions League success, but his hunger did not subside and, in 2001, he became the first manager to win three consecutive league championships in England. Sir Alex did announce his intention to retire in 2002, but changed his mind. In the Champions League, United had to wait another nine years for another final appearance and, in the Luzhniki Stadium, Moscow, on 21 May 2008, United won it for the third time, defeating Chelsea in the first-ever all-English European Cup final, this coming just ten days after they had achieved their tenth Premiership title. Sir Alex guided United to an 11th title in 2008–09 as well as League Cup success, but they lost the UEFA Champions League final to Barcelona. United won a fourth League Cup the following season and in 2010–11 United won a record 19th English League title but again United lost out to Barcelona in the Champions League final. Ferguson finally retired in 2012–13 after securing a 20th League title.

Did You Know That?
Sir Alex is the only modern manager to have won the league title in both Scotland (Aberdeen) and England (Manchester United).

❧ ALL OVER FOR OLE ❧

On 28 August 2007, just 17 days after the 2007–08 Premiership season kicked off, injury forced Manchester United's Ole Gunnar Solskjaer to retire from football. Solskjaer joined United from his local club in Norway, Molde, in 1996 for a bargain £1.5 million. He went on to etch his name in the Old Trafford history books, most famously scoring United's winning goal in the 1999 Champions League final. During his 11 years at Old Trafford the ever-popular Norwegian international won six Premier League championship winners' medals and two FA Cup winners' medals plus the UEFA Champions League. He made 366 appearances for the Red Devils and found the back of the net 126 times, including a goal on his debut as a substitute against Blackburn Rovers.

❧ MERRY-GO-ROUND AT THE BRIDGE ❧

In January 1993, Chelsea sacked their manager Ian Porterfield and brought in 1970s Chelsea legend David Webb from Southend United in his place. At the end of the season Webb was not invited to stay on at Stamford Bridge and Glenn Hoddle was appointed the Blues' new manager. Hoddle had been the manager of Swindon Town in season 1992–93 and had guided the Robins to promotion to the Premiership via a 4–3 Division One play-off victory over Leicester City. It was the first time Swindon had reached English football's top division.

❧ END OF AN ERA AT HIGHBURY ❧

The 2005–06 season was Arsenal's final season at Arsenal Stadium, Highbury. And the Gunners gave the old stadium a rousing send-off, winning their final game there 4–1 against Wigan Athletic. Thierry Henry scored a hat-trick in the game and kissed the grass at the final whistle. In the summer of 2006 the Gunners moved a short distance to their new 60,000-capacity, all-seater Emirates Stadium.

❧ PSYCHO CAN'T SAVE FOREST ❧

Following the departure of Frank Clark on 19 December 1996, Nottingham Forest appointed 34-year-old defender Stuart Pearce as their player-manager on a temporary basis. However, the former England defender, nicknamed "Psycho", could not save Forest from the drop. They finished the season in bottom position. Pearce resigned as manager in March and was replaced by Dave Bassett.

♟ PREMIER STADIUMS IN 2012–13 ♟

Team	Stadium	Capacity
Manchester United	Old Trafford	76,212
Arsenal	Emirates Stadium	60,355
Newcastle United	St James' Park	52,387
Sunderland	Stadium of Light	49,000
Manchester City	Etihad Stadium	47,726
Liverpool	Anfield	45,362
Aston Villa	Villa Park	42,788
Chelsea	Stamford Bridge	42,055
Everton	Goodison Park	40,157
Tottenham Hotspur	White Hart Lane	36,310
West Ham United	Upton Park	35,303
Southampton	St Mary's	32,689
Stoke City	Britannia Stadium	28,383
Norwich City	Carrow Road	27,033
West Bromwich Albion	The Hawthorns	26,500
Fulham	Craven Cottage	25,700
Wigan Athletic	DW Stadium	25,138
Reading	Madejski Stadium	24,161
Swansea City	Liberty Stadium	20,532
Queens Park Rangers	Loftus Road	20,000

♟ MIDDLE EASTLANDS ♟

In September 2008, the deposed Prime Minister of Thailand, Thaksin Shinawatra sold his ownership of Manchester City to the Abu Dhabi United Group. This instantly turned City into one of the world's richest clubs and they soon broke the British transfer record by paying £32.5 million to Real Madrid for Robinho. The big spending finally paid off in 2012, when City won the title for the first time since 1968.

♟ HOUDINI ACT FAILS ♟

Having narrowly avoided relegation form the Premier League at the end of the 1992–93 season on goal difference, Oldham Athletic suffered relegation 12 months later to end their three-year stint in the top flight. Whereas most clubs would have sacked their manager, the Latics continued to place their faith in Joe Royle, who at the time was the longest-serving manager in any of the four English divisions (having served at Oldham for 12 years).

❧ TWO OUTTA THREE AIN'T BAD ❧

Aston Villa beat Manchester United 3–1 in the 1994 League Cup final at Wembley to deny the Red Devils a unique Treble of Premier League championship, FA Cup and League Cup. Villa's League Cup triumph earned them a UEFA Cup place for the 1994–95 season although they only finished tenth in the Premiership, and it was a sweet victory for their manager Ron Atkinson, who had been sacked by Manchester United in November 1986 to make way for Alex Ferguson. It was also the second time one of Atkinson's teams denied Fergie the League Cup, during his reign at Sheffield Wednesday he masterminded a 1–0 victory over United in the 1991 final at Wembley.

❧ GONGS FOR FRENCH DUO ❧

In the 2003 Queen's Birthday Honours List the Arsenal manager, Arsene Wenger, and the Liverpool manager, Gerard Houllier, were awarded honorary OBEs for their services to British football.

❧ WHEN 22 BECAME 20 ❧

The 1994–95 Premiership season was the last season in which the league comprised 22 teams. Prior to the start of the campaign the Football Association had decided to reduce the Premier League to 20 teams for season 1995–96. Consequently this meant that the traditional three-up, three-down system was replaced – for one season only – with a two-up, four-down format. Ipswich Town finished the 1994–95 season rooted to the bottom of the Premiership, having achieved seven wins, while Leicester City finished second from bottom (six wins), Norwich City finished third from bottom (ten wins) and the fourth relegation place went to Crystal Palace (11 wins).

❧ TOO HUNGRY FOR SUCCESS? ❧

In February 2008, Tottenham Hotspur manager Juande Ramos was asked how he transformed Spurs' season since his appointment in October 2007. Ramos said that the team he inherited from Martin Jol was seriously overweight and had many bad eating habits. According to Ramos, the Tottenham Hotspur squad was 100 kilograms overweight when he and his backroom team arrived at White Hart Lane. However, along with the man he employed as his fitness coach at Seville, Marcos Alvarez, the pair managed to turn fat into muscle with the results bearing testimony to their dietary success.

❧ ASTON VILLA PREMIER LEAGUE FANTASY XI ❧

1
Brad
FRIEDEL

2
J.
LLOYD-SAMUEL

6
Ogo
EHIOGU

5
Olof
MELLBERG

3
Steve
STAUNTON

7
Nolberto
SOLANO

4
Gareth
BARRY
(capt.)

8
Lee
HENDRIE

9
Darius
VASSELL

10
Dwight
YORKE

11
Gabriel
AGBONLAHOR

Substitutes

Shay *GIVEN* • Gareth *SOUTHGATE* • Dean *SAUNDERS* • Andy *TOWNSEND* •
Andreas *WEIMANN* • Ray *HOUGHTON* • Kevin *RICHARDSON*

Manager

Martin *O'NEILL*

Did You Know That?

Aston Villa's most successful manager is George Ramsay. He collected six
league championships and six FA Cups between 1884 andd 1926.

❧ OWEN WINS BALLON D'OR ❧

In 2001 Michael Owen became the first Liverpool player to win
the coveted European Player of the Year award. Commonly referred
to as the "Ballon d'Or" (Golden Ball), it was established in 1956
by *France Football*, a French football magazine, and is awarded
to the footballer deemed to have been the best overall player in
European football during the year. At first only European nationals
playing in Europe qualified, but since 1995 all footballers playing
in Europe have been eligible for the award, regardless of their
birthplace. The winner is chosen by a vote of European football
journalists, one from each of UEFA's member nations. Voters select
their top-five players in order of preference, and points are assigned
to each player, descending from five points for a first-place vote to
one for a fifth-place vote.

✄ PREMIERSHIP TALK (6) ✄

"When he said that about Leeds ... I would love it if we beat them.
Love it."
*Newcastle United manager **Kevin Keegan***'s rant at Alex Ferguson on Sky
Sports, April 1996*

✄ TOP GUN HENRY ✄

During the 2005–06 season Arsenal's Thierry Henry scored 27
Premiership goals to end the season as the league's top goalscorer.
Amazingly, Henry scored one more goal than the entire Sunderland
team managed in the Premiership over their 38 games.

✄ FROM RAGS TO RICHES ✄

Blackburn Rovers won the 1994–95 Premier League to claim their
first championship success since 1913–14. The team bankrolled by
Jack Walker's millions and managed by Kenny Dalglish clinched
the title on the final day of the season – ironically at Liverpool, the
club where Dalglish enjoyed success both as a player and manager.
Despite losing 2–1 to Liverpool they still managed to win the title,
as Manchester United failed to win at West Ham United, managing
only a 1–1 draw. Jack Walker had taken over as chairman of Blackburn
Rovers in 1991, when they were struggling in Division Two and
dreaming of past glories. Rovers had not played in the top flight of
English football since 1966, the year England won the World Cup,
when they finished bottom of the First Division. Indeed, they had not
won a major trophy since 1928, when they collected the FA Cup, but
Jack Walker's money changed the course of their history.

✄ THE REEBOK STADIUM ✄

In the 1997–98 season, Bolton Wanderers welcomed Premiership
football to their new 27,000-capacity, all-seater Reebok Stadium.

✄ RAFA APPOINTED ✄

On 16 June 2004, Rafael Benitez, the former coach of Valencia,
replaced the sacked Gerard Houllier as the manager of Liverpool.
Many Liverpool fans were left stunned with the board's decision to
get rid of the man who won four cup competitions, including three
in one season, during his six-year term as the boss at Anfield.

❧ FINAL PREMIERSHIP TABLE 1996–97 ❧

Pos Team	P	W	D	L	F	A	Pts
1. Manchester United (C)	38	21	12	5	76	44	75
2. Newcastle United	38	19	11	8	73	40	68
3. Arsenal	38	19	11	8	62	32	68
4. Liverpool	38	19	11	8	62	37	68
5. Aston Villa	38	17	10	11	47	34	61
6. Chelsea	38	16	11	11	58	55	59
7. Sheffield Wednesday	38	14	15	9	50	51	57
8. Wimbledon	38	15	11	12	49	46	56
9. Leicester City	38	12	11	15	46	54	47
10. Tottenham Hotspur	38	13	7	18	44	51	46
11. Leeds United	38	11	13	14	28	38	46
12. Derby County	38	11	13	14	45	58	46
13. Blackburn Rovers	38	9	15	14	42	43	42
14. West Ham United	38	10	12	16	39	48	42
15. Everton	38	10	12	16	44	57	42
16. Southampton	38	10	11	17	50	56	41
17. Coventry City	38	9	14	15	38	54	41
18. Sunderland (R)	38	10	10	18	35	53	40
19. Middlesbrough (R)	38	10	12	16	51	60	39*
20. Nottingham Forest (R)	38	6	16	16	31	59	34

Middlesbrough had three points deducted for failing to fulfil a fixture.

❧ A UNIQUE SET OF DOUBLES ❧

Ian Wright (Crystal Palace & Arsenal 1991–92) and Teddy Sheringham (Nottingham Forest & Tottenham Hotspur 1992–93) are the only players to have won the Golden Boot award for finishing as top goalscorer in English foorball's top flight (First Division or Premier League) in a season during which they changed clubs. Following Wright's 29 league goals in the First Division in season 1991–92 (four for Palace and 25 for Arsenal) Sheringham scored 22 Premier League goals in season 1992–93 (one for Forest and 21 for Spurs).

❧ TRACTOR BOYS RUN OUT OF GROUND ❧

Just one season after winning the Premier League Manager of the Year Award for guiding Ipswich Town to fifth place in the 2000–01 Premier League, George Burley saw his Tractor Boys relegated to Division One. Ipswich finished 18th in the 2001–02 Premiership table, four points behind Sunderland.

❧ 900 PERCENT INCREASE ❧

On the opening day of the inaugural Premiership campaign in 1992–93 a total of 11 foreign-born players represented the 22 clubs. On the opening day of the 2007–08 Premier League season the figure had risen to 112 players from 20 clubs.

❧ UNITED'S DOUBLE YEAR ❧

In 1994, Manchester United retained the Premier League title, the first sponsored by Carling, and also won the FA Cup, beating Chelsea 4–0 at Wembley Stadium in the 1994 final to win the coveted Double. United became only the sixth club to achieve the Double of league championship and FA Cup following Preston North End (1889), Aston Villa (1897), Tottenham Hotspur (1961), Arsenal (1971) and Liverpool (1986).

❧ UNLUCKY SEVEN FOR BORO ❧

Arsenal recorded the biggest Premier League win of the 2005–06 season, a 7–0 thumping of Middlesbrough on 14 January 2006. The Gunners goalscorers on the day were Thierry Henry (with three) and Phillippe Senderos, Robert Pires, Gilberto Silva and Alexander Hleb with one each.

❧ SAINTS SAVE THEMSELVES ❧

Southampton found themselves in the relegation zone all through the 1998–99 season – until April, when they hit a good run of form that ultimately helped them finish 17th in the Premiership table, one place away from dropping into Division One.

❧ POMPEY GO UP ❧

The three teams promoted from the First Division to the Premier League at the end of the 2002–03 season were Portsmouth (First Division champions), Leicester City (runners-up) and Wolverhampton Wanderers (play-off winners).

❧ PREMIERSHIP TALK (7) ❧

"There is no pressure at the top. The pressure's being second or third."
*Chelsea manager **Jose Mourinho***

❧ SUPERMAN PULLS HIS SHORTS DOWN ❧

When Manchester City's Stephen Ireland scored a rocket of a volley in the 67th minute to give his side a 1–0 Premiership home win over Sunderland on 5 November 2007 he celebrated by pulling down his shorts. He had a pair of Superman pants on beneath his shorts. However, his antics would undoubtedly be looked at by the FA. The 21-year-old Ireland had already courted controversy back in September when he admitted lying about the reason for his withdrawal from the Republic of Ireland squad to face the Czech Republic, claiming his grandmother had died. It was later discovered that, much to Ireland's embarrassment, both of his grandmothers were still very much alive ... and none too pleased with the antics of their grandson.

❧ TROTTERS BREAK PIGGY BANK ❧

At the start of the 1997–98 season newly promoted Bolton Wanderers paid a club record £3.5 million for Wimbledon striker Dean Holdsworth. However, Holdsworth could not prevent the Trotters dropping straight back into Division One, although their fate was not decided until the final day of the season, when they went down on goal difference.

❧ ERIC'S BUDDY ❧

In December 1995, Manchester United had a serious injury crisis resulting in the team being bereft of experienced defenders. Alex Ferguson signed William Prunier, a friend of Eric Cantona, who had won a cap for France in 1992, on loan from Bordeaux. Prunier made his debut for United in their 2–1 home win over Queen's Park Rangers on 30 December 1995, but played just one more time for the Old Trafford side, two days later in a 4–1 defeat away to Tottenham Hotspur on New Year's Day 1996, before packing his bags to go back to France.

❧ COTTAGERS ALMOST LEFT RED-FACED ❧

In the 2005–06 season Fulham looked in danger of becoming only the third club in the 14-year history of the Premier League to go through an entire Premiership campaign without recording an away win. However, a 2–1 win over Manchester City at Eastlands on the penultimate weekend spared their blushes.

❧ CHELSEA PREMIER LEAGUE FANTASY XI ❧

1
Petr
CECH

2
Branislav
IVANOVIC

6
John
TERRY
(capt.)

5
Marcel
DESAILLY

3
Ashley
COLE

4
Claude
MAKELELE

7
Frank
LAMPARD Jnr.

8
Arjen
ROBBEN

9
Didier
DROGBA

10
Jimmy Floyd
HASSELBAINK

11
Gianfranco
ZOLA

Substitutes
Carlo *CUDICINI* • Paulo *FERREIRA* • Ricardo *CARVALHO* • Joe *COLE* •
Michael *ESSIEN* • Nicolas *ANELKA* • Fernando *TORRES*
Manager
Jose *MOURINHO*

Did You Know That?
Jose Mourinho has won League titles in four countries: in Portugal
(FC Porto), England, Italy (Inter Milan) and Spain (Real Madrid).

❧ THE ELITE FA CUP WINNERS' CLUB ❧

When Chelsea won the FA Cup final in 2007, Ashley Cole became
only the fifth modern player to win four FA Cup winners' medals:

Mark Hughes: 1985, 1990, 1994 (Manchester United), 1997 (Chelsea)
Roy Keane: 1994, 1996, 1999, 2004 (Manchester United)
David Seaman: 1993, 1998, 2002, 2003 (Arsenal)
Ryan Giggs: 1994, 1996, 1999, 2004 (Manchester United)
Ashley Cole: 2002, 2003, 2005 (Arsenal), 2007 (Chelsea)

Three 19th-century players, Arthur Kinnaird (The Wanderers and
Old Etonians), Charles Wollaston (The Wanderers) and Jimmy Forrest
(Blackburn Rovers) all won the FA Cup on five separate occasions. Cole
went on to add three more with Chelsea in 2009, 2010 and 2012.

✄ BLACK CATS GO TOP ✄

Sunderland, Coca-Cola Championship winners in season 2006–07, kicked off the 2007–08 Premier League season with a lunchtime fixture against Tottenham Hotspur at the Stadium of Light on 11 August 2007. Sunderland's Michael Chopra's 94th-minute goal put his team, managed by former Manchester United hero Roy Keane, top of the table. Although they did not remain at such dizzy heights for long, finishing the season in 15th place.

✄ I'M OFF! ✄

Swindon Town, managed by Glenn Hoddle, won promotion to the Premier League at the end of the 1992–93 season, but Hoddle did not manage the Robins in their first-ever season in the top flight, opting instead to take up an offer to become the player-manager of Chelsea. Chelsea finished 14th under Hoddle, but secured a place in the European Cup Winners' Cup for season 1994–95. The Blues may have lost the FA Cup final 4–0 to a rampant Manchester United, but because the Reds had already claimed the Premier League title, Chelsea took their place in the European Cup Winners' Cup. As for Swindon Town, John Gorman assumed control after Hoddle's departure, but they were relegated after finishing bottom of the table. They have never returned to the Premiership.

✄ HEART SCARE ✄

During the 2001–02 season Liverpool manager Gerard Houllier underwent emergency heart surgery after complaining about chest pains during the match against Leeds United at Anfield. The Liverpool manager was advised to rest, and assistant manager Phil Thompson took temporary charge of the Anfield outfit. However, the former Liverpool captain's spell in control of the club resulted in controversy when he sold Kop idol Robbie Fowler to Leeds United for £11 million.

✄ KEEGAN OFFERS TO QUIT ✄

Prior to the start of the 1996–97 season Kevin Keegan offered his resignation as Newcastle United manager. The Magpies had been hot favourites to win the 1995–96 Premier League title, only to be overhauled by Manchester United. The board persuaded Super Kev to stay, but five months later, in January 1997, Keegan quit.

❧ HARROD'S OWNER SHOPS FOR PLAYERS ❧

After Fulham won promotion to the Premier League in May 2001, the club's flamboyant chairman Mohammed Al Fayed, owner of the famous Harrod's store in London, boasted that his team could win the Premiership crown. The 2001–02 season was the Cottagers' first campaign in the top flight for 33 years, but in spite of the signings of Steve Marlet and Edwin van der Sar they could finish no higher than 13th in the table. There was speculation that Al Fayed would swoop for England captain and Manchester United midfielder David Beckham, but not even his money could not prise Becks away from Old Trafford. Fulham finished 43 points adrift of champions Arsenal.

❧ THIRD PLACE RECORD ❧

In season 2007–08, Arsenal amassed 83 points from their 38 games, but still finished third in the Premiership, behind Manchester United and Chelsea, It was a record points total for a third-placed team.

❧ A GAME EVERY WEEK ❧

Selhurst Park hosted a Premiership game almost every week during the 1994–95 and 1997–98 seasons. Wimbledon were tenants at Crystal Palace's stadium throughout their Premiership tenure and their landlords had two one-season spells in English football's top flight.

❧ SEMI-FINAL SPECIALISTS ❧

When Chelsea reached the final of the 2012–13 UEFA Europa League, they achieved something no other team had done in the history of the Premier League. They had won semi-finals in six different domestic and international competitions (most recently):

- ❖ 2012–13 .... FIFA Club World Cup ❖
- ❖ 2011–12 .... UEFA Champions League ❖
- ❖ 2012–13 .... UEFA Europa League ❖
- ❖ 1997–98 ..... UEFA European Cup Winners Cup ❖
- ❖ 2011–12 .... FA Cup ❖
- ❖ 2007–08 .... Football League Cup ❖

The Blues have done well in cup finals too as, including the Premiership, UEFA Super Cup, FA Community Shield and Full Members Cup, the only competition Chelsea have not won is the FIFA Club World Cup.

❧ KEEPING THE SHIRT ON HIS BACK ❧

On 10 November 2007, Newcastle United's new billionaire owner Mike Ashley decided to watch the 138th Tyne-Wear derby with the Geordie fans behind the goal at Sunderland's Stadium of Light rather than cause offence by wearing his Newcastle United shirt in the Sunderland directors' box. Ashley had been advised by Sunderland that if he wore his jersey it would be regarded as a provocative gesture. The match ended in a 1–1 draw.

❧ UNITED'S 2006–07 TROPHY SWEEP ❧

In a season during which Manchester United claimed their ninth FA Premier League title, a number of other awards also went to the Old Trafford outfit. Cristiano Ronaldo enjoyed the best season of his life, winning the sextuple of PFA Players' Player of the Year, PFA Young Player of the Year, PFA Fans' Player of the Year, Barclays Premiership Player of the Season, Football Writers' Association Player of the Year and a place in the FA Premier League Team of the Year (eight of the 11 selected were United players). Ryan Giggs was presented with the Barclays Premiership Merit Award in recognition of his record of nine Premier League titles, while the man who guided United to their nine Premiership crowns, Sir Alex Ferguson, was named Barclays Manager of the Season.

❧ GRASSHOPPER REFUSED WORK PERMIT ❧

In 1997, Christian Gross replaced Gerry Francis as the manager of Tottenham Hotspur. Gross left his job as coach of Grasshoppers Zurich in Switzerland to take up his appointment at White Hart Lane and attempted to bring with him to London his right-hand man at Grasshoppers, fitness coach Fritz Schmid. However, Schmid was refused a work permit by the British authorities and therefore had to remain in Zurich. When, eleven months later, Gross was sacked and replaced by George Graham, he returned to Switzerland to take charge of FC Basel, and by the end of the 2006–07 season he had guided the team to three Swiss championships and three Swiss Cups.

❧ SKY BLUES FALL IN ON REDS ❧

On 19 December 1992 Liverpool travelled to Highfield Road and were soundly beaten 5–1 by Coventry City. It remains the Reds' record defeat in the Premier League to date.

⚹ TOTTENHAM GO DUTCH ⚹

In September 2003, Tottenham Hotspur sacked Glenn Hoddle and replaced him in the managerial hot seat with the club's director of football, David Pleat. Pleat took over as temporary manager until the end of the season when a permanent appointment was given to Jacques Santini, formerly the French national coach. Santini's tenure at White Hart Lane only lasted for five months, however, before he was replaced with Spurs' assistant first-team coach, Martin Jol.

⚹ WALKERS STADIUM ⚹

In November 2000, Leicester City announced that the club would move to a brand-new all-seater stadium, the Walkers Stadium, with capacity for 32,000 spectators at the beginning of the 2003–04 season. The new stadium was built next to Leicester City's old Filbert Street ground, and as it turned out the club were able to move into their new home a year early in time for the start of the 2002–03 season.

⚹ THE RETURN OF THE MESSIAH ⚹

Shortly after Christain Gross succeeded Gerry Francis as the manager of Tottenham Hotspur in November 1997, his first move was to appease the continuing hostility towards the club's chairman, Alan Sugar, by bringing back a former White Hart Lane hero, Jurgen Klinsmann. At the end of the 1997–98 season, in which Spurs finished 14th in the Premiership and Klinsmann netted nine times in 15 appearances, the German striker announced that he would hang up his boots after the World Cup finals in France. Klinsmann enjoyed a highly successful playing carer before going on to coach the German national team (2004–06). He won the UEFA Cup twice (in 1991 with Inter Milan and in 1996 with Bayern Munich), won the Bundesliga with Bayern Munich in 1997, was voted German Footballer of the Year twice (1988 & 1994) and English Footballer of the Year in 1995. As a player with the German national team he won the 1990 World Cup and the 1996 European Championships in addition to a bronze medal at the 1988 Seoul Olympics.

⚹ PREMIERSHIP TALK (8) ⚹

"Young players need freedom of expression to develop as creative players... they should be encouraged to try skills without fear of failure."
Arsenal manager **Arsene Wenger**

♒ RYAN GIGGS, OBE ♒

Ryan Joseph Wilson was born in Cardiff on 29 November 1973. In July 1990 Ryan signed as a trainee with Manchester United, signing professional forms five months later. He then adopted his mother's maiden name and became Ryan Giggs. In March 1991 he made his first-team debut for United as a substitute against Everton at Old Trafford, and scored the winner against Manchester City on his full debut in May. His dazzling performances for United on their left wing earned him his first call-up to the Welsh national team in October 1991. Aged just 17 years and 321 days, he was the youngest ever Welsh international.

In 1992–93, Ryan helped United to the inaugural FA Premier League Championship. That season his peers voted him the PFA Young Player of the Year for the second season in succession – the first time a player had received the award twice. The following season a dominant United won the domestic Double of Premier League and FA Cup; two years later they repeated the feat. A fourth Premiership-winners' medal followed in 1996–97, but Ryan's finest season was 1998–99, when United became the first and, to date, only winners of the Treble of League, FA Cup and Champions League. An outstanding memory from that campaign came when Ryan scored what is considered by many to be the greatest goal in FA Cup history, a thrilling zigzag run, in United's 2–1 win over Arsenal in the epic FA Cup semi-final replay at Villa Park. In November 1999 United won the Intercontinental Cup (World Club Championship) with a 1–0 win over Palmeiras of Brazil in Tokyo and Ryan took home a brand-new Toyota Celica car after being named Man of the Match.

On 23 August 2002, he scored his 100th goal for United in their 2–2 draw with Chelsea. In May 2004, he collected his fourth FA Cup-winners' medal following United's 3–0 victory over Millwall in the Millennium Stadium, Cardiff. Ryan played for Wales 64 times and ended his international career captaining the team in a 0–0 draw with the Czech Republic in a Euro 2008 qualifying game. On 11 May 2008, the day Giggs tied Sir Bobby Charlton's United appearance record with 758, he scored the decisive second goal in the title-winning match against Wigan Athletic. Not only has Ryan played more than 900 matches for United and been alongside around 150 different team-mates at Old Trafford, in 2013, he became only the third man to appear in 1,000 senior competitive fixtures in English football. No player in English football can boast his club trophy haul: 13 Premiership crowns, four FA Cups, four League Cup, two UEFA Champions Leagues and the European Cup Winners' Cup.

Did You Know That?
Ryan captained the England Schoolboys.

✂ THERE'S ONLY ONE DAVID BETNLEY ✂

When England international David Bentley took to the Old Trafford pitch for Blackburn Rovers' Premiership game against Manchester United on 11 November 2007 his name was spelt wrongly on the back of his shirt. Someone at the Ewood Park print shop had spelt his name BETNLEY. During the game itself, Manchester United beat Blackburn Rovers 2–0 to return to the top of the Premiership.

✂ A COSTLY BUNG ✂

On 21 February 1995, George Graham, who had been in charge of Arsenal for nine years and guided them to two First Division championships, was sacked by the London club after it was discovered that he had accepted an illegal "bung" of £425,000 from a Norwegian football agent, Rune Hauge, when Arsenal purchased John Jensen and Pal Lydersen after the 1992 European Championships. Graham, a former Arsenal and Manchester United player, was also handed a one-year ban from the game by the Football Association after he admitted to accepting an "unsolicited gift". The Gunners appointed Stewart Houston as their caretaker manager until the end of the season, after which Bruce Rioch took over.

✂ DOUBLE FOR GIGGSY ✂

Ryan Giggs, aged 19, was named the PFA Young Player of the Year in the 1992–93 season for the second successive year. Paul McGrath (Aston Villa), aged 34, was voted the PFA Players' Player of the Year, while 32-year-old Chris Waddle of Sheffield Wednesday collected the Football Writers' Player of the Year award.

✂ GOLDEN BALLS JOINS *LOS GALACTICOS* ✂

At the end of the 2002–03 season the newly crowned Premier League champions Manchester United sold one of their most prized assets, the England captain David Beckham. David, whose nicknamess included "Golden Balls", joined Real Madrid, nicknamed *los galacticos*, for a staggering £25 million.

✂ SEVEN TO SEVEN ✂

In the 1993–94 Premiership season, Sheffield Wednesday finished in seventh place for the second successive year.

⚒ FINAL PREMIERSHIP TABLE 1997–98 ⚒

Pos Team	P	W	D	L	F	A	Pts
1. Arsenal (C)	38	23	9	6	68	33	78
2. Manchester United	38	23	8	7	73	26	77
3. Liverpool	38	18	11	9	68	42	65
4. Chelsea	38	20	3	15	71	43	63
5. Leeds United	38	17	8	13	57	46	59
6. Blackburn Rovers	38	16	10	12	57	52	58
7. Aston Villa	38	17	6	15	49	48	57
8. West Ham United	38	16	8	14	56	57	56
9. Derby County	38	16	7	15	52	49	55
10. Leicester City	38	13	14	11	51	41	53
11. Coventry City	38	12	16	10	46	44	52
12. Southampton	38	14	6	18	50	55	48
13. Newcastle United	38	11	11	16	35	44	44
14. Tottenham Hotspur	38	11	11	16	44	56	44
15. Wimbledon	38	10	14	14	34	46	44
16. Sheffield Wednesday	38	12	8	18	52	67	44
17. Everton	38	9	13	16	41	56	40
18. Bolton Wanderers (R)	38	9	13	16	41	61	40
19. Barnsley (R)	38	10	5	23	37	82	35
20. Crystal Palace (R)	38	8	9	21	37	71	33

⚒ ERIKSSON ENDS GOAL DROUGHT ⚒

In Sven-Goran Eriksson's first home game in charge of Manchester City, against Derby County on 15 August 2007, the team won 1–0 but, more importantly, Michael Johnson's winner ended a 227-day goal drought for City at home.

⚒ NEW BACKERS ⚒

From the beginning of the 1993-94 season the Premier League was sponsored by Carling Breweries and was officially named the FA Carling Premier League.

⚒ EUROPEAN ROVERS ⚒

For the second successive season Blackburn Rovers qualified for the UEFA Cup thanks to a sixth-place finish in the 2002–03 Premier League table. In season 2001–02 they qualified for the UEFA Cup as League Cup winners.

A RECORD TUMBLES

Derby County managed only one win in their 38 Premiership games in 2007–08 – 1–0 at home to Newcastle United on 17 September – and ended up with just 11 points, the lowest total in Premier League history. Amazingly, the Rams finished 25 points from safety and a staggering 76 adrift of champions Manchester United. The previous record, set by Sunderland in 2005–06, was 15 points.

BIG OGGI HANGS UP HIS GLOVES

At the end of the 1999–2000 season Coventry City's goalkeeper, Steve Ogrizovic, retired from the game after 17 years with the club and 24 years as a professional footballer. Forty-three-year-old Ogrizovic was the last surviving member of Coventry's famous 1987 FA Cup-winning side still at Highfield Road. Steve holds the club record at Coventry City for the most appearances as a player with 601 in all competitions (504 league games) and is one of a select band of goalkeepers who have scored a goal directly from a goal-kick (in a 2–2 draw at Sheffield Wednesday on 12 October 1986).

THE WEMBLEY OF THE NORTH

At the end of the 1994–95 season, Leeds United finished fifth in the Premiership and announced ambitious new plans to build a new 65,000 all-seater stadium they dubbed "The Wembley of the North". The plans never came to fruition.

CHANGES AT THE HELM

In the summer of 1995 Arsenal appointed Bruce Rioch as their new manager. Rioch had just taken Bolton Wanderers into the Premiership after a 15-year exile from of the top flight. Bolton, meanwhile, appointed Roy McFarland and Colin Todd as joint managers, but McFarland was sacked on New Year's Day 1996, leaving Todd in sole charge. Alan Ball took charge at Manchester City, while David Pleat (Luton Town) replaced Trevor Francis at Sheffield Wednesday.

ARSENAL'S UNWANTED TREBLE

In 2000–01 Arsenal finished runners-up to Manchester United in the Premiership for a third consecutive season. However, in both 1997–98 and 2001–02, it was the Gunners who were crowned champions.

♚ PREMIERSHIP THREATENS ENGLAND ♛

In an interview with BBC1's *Inside Sport* programme on 3 September 2007, Sir Trevor Brooking, the Football Association's director of development, said that England's chances of achieving success on the pitch were in jeopardy. The former West Ham United and England international cited the influx of foreign players into the Premier League as the primary reason why England lack experienced players in key areas.

Sir Trevor said: "I don't think you can underestimate it. It's a major concern. Last year about 40 per cent of starting XIs in the Premier League were English. And with all the buying that has gone on over the summer that will probably fall to under a third. Will there be first-team opportunities for some of our youngsters aged between 17 and 21? If you look at Italy when they won the last World Cup, I think they had over 70 per cent of their league made up of domestic players. Spain, France, Holland, they're all up there, too. Germany aren't much better than us, but we're the lowest. The more that goes down, and the pool of choice reduces, we must come under pressure. In ten years' time you don't want us just being pleased to qualify for tournaments."

Research by *Inside Sport* showed that:

* 76 per cent of the starting XIs that played on the first weekend of the inaugural Premier League season in 1992–93 were English compared with 37 per cent on the first weekend of the 2007–08 season.
* Only 10 per cent (23 players) of the starting XIs in 1992–93 were from outside the UK compared with 56 per cent (123) in 2007–08.
* After the opening four weekends of the 2007–08 Premier League season non-English players had scored 69 per cent of the 118 goals (including two of the three own goals).
* Of those 118 goals scored, only nine were scored by seven different English forwards.
* According to the latest Deloitte figures for disclosed transfer fees, spending by Premier League clubs rose from £333 million in 2006 to £531 million in 2007.
* More than 50 per cent of the money spent by Premier League clubs for the 2007–08 Premiership campaign was handed over to non-English clubs.

♚ GUNNERS' LUCKY 13 ♛

The Premier League title clinched by Arsenal in 2004 was their third Premiership crown and their 13th championship overall.

☙ ARSENAL'S MILLENNIUM MAN ❧

When Emmanuel Adebayor scored Arsenal's second goal in their
3–1 win over Reading at the Madejski Stadium on 12 November
2007, it was the Gunners' 1,000th Premier League goal. They were
now one of only two clubs – along with Manchester United – to have
scored 1,000 or more goals in the Premiership. The Red Devils were
on 1,136 at the time, having reached their thousandth goal during
the 2005–06 season.

☙ CAPTAIN MARVEL LEAVES CHAMPIONS ❧

Bryan Robson left the Double winners Manchester United at the
end of the 1993–94 season to take up the post of player-manager
at Middlesbrough in Division One. Robbo, or "Captain Marvel" as
he was nicknamed by the United and England fans, had spent 13
years at Old Trafford and won just about every honour in the game,
including two Premier League titles, three FA Cups, one League
Cup, one European Cup Winners' Cup and the European Super Cup.
Robson appointed his former United team-mate, Viv Anderson, as
his assistant manager.

☙ THE GLASGOW CONNECTION ❧

On 13 March 2002, Everton sacked manager Walter Smith and
replaced the former Glasgow Rangers manager with a former
Glasgow Celtic player, David Moyes. Moyes left his post as manager
of Preston North End to take the helm at Goodison Park and
managed to steer the troubled club clear of relegation, finishing
15th in the table, 37 points behind their bitter rivals Liverpool, who
finished runners-up to champions Arsenal.

☙ ABLETT DOUBLES UP ❧

Gary Ablett won an FA Cup-winners' medal with Liverpool in 1989
and repeated the achievement with Everton in 1995.

☙ CROSSING THE BITTER DIVIDE ❧

At the start of the 2001–02 season, Arsenal unveiled their new
signing, Sol Campbell, who moved across London from rivals
Tottenham Hotspur on a free transfer. Campbell helped the Gunners
to the Double in his first season with the club.

⚘ PREMIERSHIP TALK (9) ⚘

"There were one or two stray passes and they were getting on players' backs. It's out of order. I don't think some of them can even spell football, let alone understand it. Away from home our fans are fantastic. But at home they have a few drinks and probably the prawn sandwiches, and they don't realize what's going on out on the pitch."

Roy Keane after United's 1–0 win over Dynamo Kiev in the UEFA Champions League

⚘ ERIC'S KUNG-FU ATTACK ⚘

On 25 January 1995, Manchester United visited the capital for a Premiership game against Crystal Palace at Selhurst Park. The game ended in a 1–1 draw, but what happened during the match had a profound effect on the final destination of the Premiership trophy for the 1994–95 season. Cantona, United's enigmatic French striker and the reigning PFA Players' Player of the Year, was sent off and was verbally abused by a home fan on his way to the dressing-rooms. The red mist descended and Eric jumped, kung-fu style, into the crowd and lashed out at the foul-mouthed Eagles fan. A huge furore followed, as well as criminal charges, resulting in Cantona being banned by the Premier League for eight months, fined £20,000 and sentenced to two weeks in prison, which was subsequently reduced to 120 hours' community service on appeal. Without the inspirational Cantona, United narrowly missed out on winning the domestic Double for the second season in a row and their third successive Premiership crown, finishing one point behind Blackburn Rovers, and losing 1–0 to Everton in the 1995 FA Cup final.

⚘ TWO HISTORIC LIONS ⚘

On 7 June 2006, Gareth Southgate was appointed Middlesbrough manager after Steve McClaren took up his new role as England coach. Southgate had been a Boro player from 2001 up until his new appointment. Prior to joining Boro, Southgate played for Aston Villa (1995–2001) and, on 7 October 2000, Southgate and his Villa team-mate Gareth Barry, became the only two players to have played in England's last-ever international at the old Wembley Stadium (a 1–0 loss to Germany) and in the last FA Cup final under the famous Twin Towers (Villa lost the 2000 FA Cup final 1–0 to Chelsea).

⚔ A CENTURY AT THE WRONG END ⚔

During the 1993–94 Premiership season, Swindon Town won just five games, drew 15 and lost 22 to make an immediate return to Division One. The Robins not only found it hard to score goals, managing only 47 from their 42 games, but leaked them like a tap at the back, conceding 100 goals. Also relegated were Oldham Athletic, who only avoided the drop the previous season on goal difference, and Sheffield United.

⚔ THE £¼ BILLION TEAM ⚔

The Chelsea team that won the 2004–05 Premier League title was, at the time, the most expensive football team ever created in British football. The team cost an estimated £250 million to assemble and included star purchases such as Wayne Bridge, Ricardo Carvalho, Petr Cech, Joe Cole, Didier Drogba, Paulo Ferreira, Eidur Gudjohnsen, Frank Lampard and Claude Makele. However, The Manchester City squad in 2012–13 cost a staggering £312.05 million to assemble.

⚔ THE SAINTS' MIRACLE WORKER ⚔

In 1997–98 Dave Jones, whose previous management experience had not seen him manage a team above Division Two, guided Southampton to a respectable 12th place in the Premier League.

⚔ OLDEST PREMIER LEAGUE MANAGER ⚔

In September 1999, Ruud Gullit quit his position as manager of Newcastle United after the Geordies lost four of their opening five Premiership games and was replaced by the former England manager Sir Bobby Robson. At the time Sir Bobby was 66 years old, making him the oldest manager in the history of the Premiership (he was 71 when he left the Geordies in 2004). Newcastle United finished the 1999–2000 season 11th in the table, four places below their bitter rivals Sunderland, who had only won promotion the previous season.

⚔ PLAYERS PAY FOR FANS' TRAVEL ⚔

On 24 November 2007, the Reading players subsidised their fans' trip to Manchester to see the team play Manchester City in the Premiership. The Royals squad donated £5,000 towards the costs of providing coaches to take fans to Eastlands. City won the match 2–1.

☕ LIVERPOOL PREMIER LEAGUE FANTASY XI ☕

1
Bruce
GROBBELAAR

2
Glen
JOHNSON

5
Jamie
CARRAGHER

6
Sami
HYYPIA

3
Josee
ENRIQUE

7
Steve
McMANAMAN

4
Xabi
ALONSO

8
Steven
GERRARD
(capt.)

9
Ian
RUSH

10
Robbie
FOWLER

11
John
BARNES

Substitutes
Pepe *REINA* • John Arne *RIISE* • Mark *WRIGHT* • Xavi *ALONSO* •
Jamie *REDKNAPP* • Luis *SUAREZ* • Michael *OWEN*

Manager
Rafa *BENITEZ*

Did You Know That?
Jamie Carragher, who retired in 2013, holds the record for the most appearances in European competition for Liverpool.

☕ SIX APPEAL ☕

Cristiano Ronaldo's first hat-trick for Manchester United helped the champions to a comfortable 6–0 win over Newcastle United at Old Trafford in the Premiership on 12 January 2008. Amazingly, all six United goals came in the second half, when the managerless Geordies were totally outclassed in all areas of the pitch.

☕ A BARN FULL OF OWLS ☕

In October 1997, Sheffield Wednesday sacked their manager David Pleat and brought in Ron Atkinson as caretaker manager. At the end of the 1997–98 season, after guiding the Owls to 16th position and Premiership safety, Big Ron was replaced with Barnsley's outgoing manager Danny Wilson, a former Owls player.

✂ AN EARLY BATH ✂

Dave Kitson came on as a substitute for Reading against Manchester United at Old Trafford in their opening game of the 2007–08 season and was quickly given an early bath – it was the first Premiership sending-off of the season. The game ended 0–0.

✂ AN EXPENSIVE PAIR OF GLOVES ✂

Prior to the start of the 1993–94 season Tim Flowers became Britain's most expensive goalkeeper when he left Southampton to join Kenny Dalglish's Blackburn Rovers in a deal worth £2.5 million.

✂ SURVIVAL SUNDAY ✂

Sunday, 15 May 2005, was the last day of the 2004–05 Premiership season. West Bromwich Albion sat at the foot of the table, and the other two relegation places were occupied by Southampton and Crystal Palace, both precariously placed one point above the Baggies. Norwich City occupied the last safe spot, two points above the foot of the table. This final day of the Premierhip season was unique in that, for the first time in the league's 13-year history, no club had been assured of relegation Southampton lost 2–1 at home to Manchester United and were relegated. Norwich City, with their fate in their own hands, lost 6–0 to Fulham at Craven Cottage and also went down. Crystal Palace were leading 2–1 at Charlton Athletic, with just eight minutes separating them from Premiership survival. But they conceded an equalizer to Jonathan Fortune, which was enough to send the Eagles back to the Championship. Meanwhile West Bromwich Albion beat Portsmouth 2–0 at the Hawthorns to avoid the drop.

✂ TOP HAMMER ✂

Prior to the start of the 1994–95 season, West Ham United sacked manager and former hero Billy Bonds – their 1975 and 1980 FA Cup-winning captain. His replacement, Harry Redknapp, another former player, acted swiftly to deflect any flak coming his way by bringing Hammers hero Tony Cottee back to the Boleyn Ground from Everton after a six-year absence. Redknapp, who had been linked with a return to take charge of his old club Bournemouth, guided the London club to 14th in the Premiership.

⚘ EVERTON PREMIER LEAGUE FANTASY XI ⚘

1
Neville
SOUTHALL

2
Phil
NEVILLE

6
Joleon
LESCOTT

5
Dave
WATSON

3
Leighton
BAINES

7
Mikel
ARTETA

4
Marouane
FELLAINI

8
Leon
OSMAN

9
Tim
CAHILL

10
Duncan
FERGUSON

11
Nikica
JELAVIC

Substitutes
Tim *HOWARD* • Andy *HINCHCLIFFE* • Phil *JAGIELKA* •
David *UNSWORTH* • Thomas *GRAVESEN* • Steven *PIENAAR* • *YAKUBU*

Manager
David *MOYES*

Did You Know That?
David Moyes had to pay a club record fee of £11.25 million to secure the services of Yakubu from Middlesbrough in the summer of 2007.

⚘ WHEN THE GUNS FAILED TO FIRE ⚘

The 1994–95 season was one of turmoil for Arsenal. George Graham was sacked over a bungs scandal and was temporarily replaced by Stewart Houston until Bruce Rioch came in at the end of the season. The Gunners, First Division winners in 1989 and 1991, could only manage 12th place in the Premiership. However, Arsenal did reach the final of the European Cup Winners' Cup for the second year in succession and faced Real Zaragoza in Paris. The game went into extra-time, and with 120 minutes shown on the game clock and the score at 1–1, a penalty shoot-out was beckoning when Nayim lobbed David Seaman from the half-way line to win the trophy for the Spaniards. To add insult to injury, Nayim, full name Mohammed Ali Amar, played for Tottenham Hotspur from 1988 to 1993.

⚜ THE WAY IT USED TO BE ⚜

Manchester United finished runners-up to Leeds United in the final season of the English First Division Championship in 1991–92, but their dominance of British football during the 1990s was just about to commence. Luton Town, Nottingham Forest and West Ham United were all relegated to the newly formed English League Division One, which replaced the former Second Division. During the season the legendary West Ham United and England captain, Bobby Moore, died of cancer aged just 51 (24 February 1993).

Ipswich Town, winners of the last-ever Second Division championship under the old system, and runners-up Middlesbrough, hit the jackpot with automatic promotion to the newly formed FA Premier League and a share of the money poured into it by BSkyB. Blackburn Rovers, managed by the legendary Glasgow Celtic, Liverpool and Scotland striker, Kenny Dalglish, won the play-off final 1–0 against Leicester City thanks to a goal from Mike Newell, a former Leicester City striker. Dalglish, backed by owner Sir Jack Walker's deep pockets, ended Rovers' 26-year absence from English football's top flight.

⚜ BRUMMIES JOIN BLACK CATS IN THE DROP ⚜

Birmingham City and West Bromwich Albion were relegated to the Coca-Cola League along with Sunderland at the end of the 2005–06 Premier League season.

⚜ OLD BIG 'EAD ⚜

In 1993 Nottingham Forest finished bottom of the inaugural FA Premier League and were relegated. Their run of six successive defeats during the season was the worst suffered by any of the Premiership's 22 clubs. It was a sad end to the Forest reign of Brian Clough, who took the decision to retire. When the man nicknamed "Old Big 'ead" took charge at the City Ground, in January 1975, Forest were a mediocre Division Two side who still looked on their two FA Cup final wins (in 1898 and 1959) as the defining moments in the club's history. Cloughie rewrote their history books, guiding them to the First Division championship in 1978, European Cup success in 1979 and again in 1980, as well as four League Cups. All but two of Forest's trophies under Clough (two League Cups) came during his first six years at the helm.

❧ FINAL PREMIERSHIP TABLE 1998–99 ❧

Pos Team	P	W	D	L	F	A	Pts
1. Manchester United (C)	38	22	13	3	80	37	79
2. Arsenal	38	22	12	4	59	17	78
3. Chelsea	38	20	15	3	57	30	75
4. Leeds United	38	18	13	7	62	34	67
5. West Ham United	38	16	9	13	46	53	57
6. Aston Villa	38	15	10	13	55	51	55
7. Liverpool	38	15	9	14	68	49	54
8. Derby County	38	13	13	12	40	45	52
9. Middlesbrough	38	12	15	11	48	54	51
10. Leicester City	38	12	13	13	40	46	49
11. Tottenham Hotspur	38	11	14	13	47	50	47
12. Sheffield Wednesday	38	13	7	18	41	42	46
13. Newcastle United	38	11	13	14	48	54	46
14. Everton	38	11	10	17	42	47	43
15. Coventry City	38	11	9	18	39	51	42
16. Wimbledon	38	10	12	16	40	63	42
17. Southampton	38	11	8	19	37	64	41
18. Charlton Athletic (R)	38	8	12	18	41	56	36
19. Blackburn Rovers (R)	38	7	14	17	38	52	35
20. Nottingham Forest (R)	38	7	9	22	35	69	30

❧ TOP CANARY ❧

At the start of the 1992–93 season, Norwich City youth team manager Mike Walker was promoted to the hot seat in place of Dave Stringer. Under Walker's guidance the Canaries made it to third place in the league and into European football in the shape of the UEFA Cup for the 1993–94 season. It would be the Canaries' first experience of European football. Eight years earlier their 1–0 win over Sunderland in the 1984–85 League Cup final guaranteed the club UEFA Cup football in the 1985–86 season. However, following the Heysel tragedy in May 1985, English clubs were banned from Europe and the Canaries missed out on their inaugural European adventure.

❧ DEN BREAKS BANK ❧

When Dennis Bergkamp joined Arsenal from Inter Milan for £7.5 million in June 1995, the fee was a new British transfer record. Bruce Rioch, the Arsenal manager, also paid close to £5 million to Sampdoria for the services of the England captain David Platt.

❧ AU REVOIR, CANTONA ❧

On 18 May 1997, the day after Manchester United were crowned Premiership champions for 1996–97, Eric Cantona dropped a bombshell on the club by announcing his retirement from playing. The enigmatic French maestro joined United in November 1992 from Leeds United for a modest £1.1 million and over the next five seasons he helped Manchester United win four Premiership titles (1992–93, 1993–94, 1995–96 and 1996–97) and two FA Cups (1994 and 1996) as well being voted PFA Player of the Year in 1994 and FWA Player of the Year in 1996. His departure left United fans everywhere heartbroken.

❧ CHAMPIONS LEAGUE BECKONING ❧

Four games into the 2007–08 Premier League season Wigan Athletic found themselves sitting third in the table – which as a final league position would be enough to secure entry to the third qualifying round of the 2008–09 UEFA Champions League campaign.

❧ LATICS GET THEIR MAN AGAIN ❧

On 19 November 2007, Steve Bruce packed his bags as manager of Birmingham City after almost six years in charge at St Andrews to take up the managerial reins at Wigan Athletic. It was the second time the former Manchester United captain managed the Latics, having been their boss for seven weeks in 2001. Dave Whelan, the chairman of Wigan Athletic, agreed to pay Birmingham City £3 million in compensation for Bruce's services. Bruce succeeded Chris Hutchings, who was sacked at the beginning of November 2007.

❧ FROM APPRENTICE TO SORCERER ❧

In early October 1998, George Graham resigned as the Leeds United manager to become Tottenham Hotspur's new boss, after the London club had sacked Christian Gross. Leicester City manager Martin O'Neill was hotly tipped to take charge of the Yorkshire club, but he stayed loyal to the Foxes. Instead, another Irishman, David O'Leary, was promoted from Leeds' assistant manager into the hot seat. While Graham went on to guide Spurs to League Cup glory in 1999, O'Leary steered Leeds to fourth place in the Premiership, and both clubs were guaranteed UEFA Cup football in the 1999–2000 season.

♕ PREMIERSHIP TALK (10) ♕

"It was a freakish incident. If I tried it 100 or a million times it couldn't happen again. If I could I would have carried on playing!"
Sir Alex Ferguson on how he kicked a boot that hit David Beckham above his eye

♕ RETURN OF THE TOON KING ♕

On 16 January 2008, Newcastle United announced that former player and former manager Kevin Keegan would make a dramatic return to manage the Magpies. The 56-year-old former England, Newcastle United, Fulham and Manchester City boss, who managed the Geordies from 1992 to 1997, made a hero's return to St James' Park as the successor to Sam Allardyce.

♕ THE KID FROM OZ ♕

In season 1999–2000 Leeds United's exciting young Australian midfielder, Harry Kewell, helped the Elland Road club to a third-place finish in the Premiership table and UEFA Champions League football the following season. Kewell's performances throughout the season earned him the PFA Young Player of the Year Award.

♕ THE LAST MAINE ROAD DERBY ♕

In the 2002–03 season, Manchester City beat Manchester United 3–1 at Maine Road in what was the last ever Manchester derby game played at Maine Road. It was also City's first win over the red half of Manchester in 13 years, during which time United had collected seven Premiership crowns. However, despite the 3–1 defeat, United went on to lift their eighth Premiership title at the end of the campaign. City in contrast finished ninth in the Premiership table and moved to their new home at Eastlands (the City of Manchester Stadium) for the start of the new season.

♕ TOFFEE GAZZA ♕

At the end of the 1999–2000 season Everton finished a disappointing 13th in the Premiership table, leading their manager Walter Smith to turn to one of his former players at Rangers to help bring the good times back to Goodison Park. Over the close season Smith managed to persuade Paul Gascoigne to leave Middlesbrough for Everton.

☙ LIVERPOOL KNOCKED OFF THER PERCH ☙

By winning the Premier League in 2010–11, Manchester United clinched their 19th top-flight title and achieveing a long-held ambition of manager Sir Alex Ferguson in deposing Liverpool as England's most successful club. Liverpool have been unable to add to their 18 titles since winning the old First Division in 1990.

☙ SWANS FLYING HIGH ☙

Swansea City became the first non-English club to play in the Premier League when they won the Championship Playoff final against Reading in May 2011. Just eight years earlier, they had come within one point of dropping out of the Football League altogether and entering the Football Conference.

☙ HOT SHOTS ☙

Chelsea won their third Premier League crown in May 2010 and set a Premiership record with their total of 103 goals. The Blues scored four times away to Bolton Wanderers and at home to Wolverhampton Wanderers and West Ham United; they bagged five at home to Blackburn Rovers and away to Portsmouth; seven at home to Sunderland, Aston Villa and Stoke City, and rounded off the season with an 8–0 thrashing of Wigan Athletic. Ivory Coast striker Didier Drogba won the Premiership Golden Boot – his second award with Chelsea – after scoring 29 goals.

☙ THE BOYS ARE BACK IN TOWN ☙

Going into the 2004–05 season Crystal Palace and Norwich City were back among the big boys after winning promotion from the Championship, along with Premier League newcomers West Bromwich Albion.

☙ CRAZY GANG DEFY THE ODDS ☙

In season 1993–94 Wimbledon, the least wealthy of all the clubs in the Premier League and a team who didn't even have a home ground (they were still renting Crystal Palace's Selhurst Park), defied the odds and finished sixth in the table to equal their highest-ever finish in the top flight. Only one London club, Arsenal (fourth), finished above the Crazy Gang.

♚ THIERRY HENRY ♚

Thierry Daniel Henry was born in Les Ulis, Essonne, a suburb of Paris, on 17 August 1977. When he was 12 years old, a scout from AS Monaco watched him score six goals in a match that his team won 6–0 and immediately signed him without even a trial. From 1990 to 1992 he was loaned out to Viry-Chatillon to gain experience, and in 1992 he also attended Clairefontaine, the French national football centre of excellence. Two years later he made his professional debut for AS Monaco, and in 1997 he made his international debut for France. During his four years in the first team at AS Monaco he scored 20 goals in 110 matches in Le Championnat, winning a league title in 1996–97. It was enough to convince the Italian giants Juventus to buy him. However, his move to Serie A did not work out, as he was usually played out of position on the right wing. In 1999 Arsene Wenger, his former manager at AS Monaco, paid £10.5 million to bring him to Arsenal as a replacement for Nicolas Anelka, who had moved on to Real Madrid.

Although Henry failed to score in his first eight games, he soon flourished in Wenger's side. In his first season with Arsenal he scored 26 goals, with the team finishing runners-up to Manchester United in the Premier League and beaten finalists in the UEFA Cup to Galatasaray. In the summer of 2000 Henry was one of a number of star French players who helped their country to victory in the European Championships. After Arsenal had finished runners-up to Manchester United in the Premiership for the third consecutive year in 2000–01, Henry's 32 goals helped the Gunners to complete the Double of Premier League and FA Cup success in season 2001–02.

In season 2002–03 Henry banged in 43 goals in all competitions for Arsenal as they retained the FA Cup. Although United reclaimed the Premiership crown, Henry collected the PFA Players' Player of the Year Award and the Football Writers' Association Footballer of the Year Award. Season 2003–04 saw Arsenal not only win back the Premiership title but also go through the entire season unbeaten, and following Patrick Vieira's departure to Juventus in 2005 Henry was made club captain. Henry led Arsenal to the UEFA Champions League final in 2006, but a year later he left for FC Barcelona, their conquerors in the final. Thierry made a brief return to Arsenal in a five-week loan deal from the New York Red Bulls in January 2010.

Did You Know That?
Thierry Henry surpassed the club's all-time goalscoring record set by Cliff Bastin, scoring 228 goals in all competitions for the Gunners.

✄ 125-UP FOR SPURS ✄

The 2007–08 season was Tottenham Hotspur's 125th year of existence.

✄ THE UNDEFEATED CHAMPIONS ✄

Arsenal, Premiership champions for the third time in season 2003–04, went through their entire league campaign of 38 matches unbeaten, matching the feat of Preston North End in 1888–89. Arsenal finished the Premiership campaign with 26 wins, 12 draws and 90 points. In 1888–89 the Lilywhites of Preston, playing in the inaugural First Division championship, ended their league campaign with 18 wins, 4 draws and 40 points (under the 2 points for a win system).

✄ THOSE EUROPEAN BLUES ✄

In season 2002–03 Chelsea finished fourth in the Premier League table, 16 points behind the champions Manchester United, and qualified for the UEFA Champions League the following season. It was the Blues' first UEFA Champions League qualification in five seasons. Back in 1955 Chelsea won the First Division and were invited to participate in the inaugural European Cup. However, the Football Association barred them from entering the competition.

✄ THE UNITED NATIONS OF FOOTBALL ✄

France has supplied in excess of 60 more players to the Premier League than any other nation, excluding Scotland, Wales, Northern Ireland and the Republic of Ireland. The top 10 are as follows (based on playing at least one Premier League match):

Rank	Country	No. of players
1.	France	158
2.	Netherlands	93
3.	Spain	65
4.	Italy	56
=5.	Norway	52
=	Sweden	52
7.	Brazil	49
8.	Denmark	48
9.	Portugal	44
10.	Australia	43

❧ THE CHELSEA JINX ❧

On 26 November 2007 Billy Davies became the sixth Premiership manager of the 2007–08 season to lose his job when he left Derby County. Davies left the Rams rooted to the foot of the table, two points adrift of the club in 19th place, following their 2–0 home defeat to Chelsea. Amazingly, two of the other five Premier League managers, Sammy Lee (Bolton Wanderers) and Chris Hutchings (Wigan Athletic), also lost their jobs after losing to Chelsea. Another former Wigan Athletic manager, Paul Jewell, took charge of Derby.

❧ THE FOREIGN INVASION BEGINS ❧

Prior to the start of the 1995–96 season, the Nottingham Forest manager Frank Clark signed Andrea Silenzi from AS Torino for £1.8 million, and he became the first Italian ever to play in the English Premier League. Silenzi failed to settle, however, making just ten league appearances without scoring. Two games into the 1996–97 season Forest loaned the Italian out to Venezia, and after making a further ten appearances for Forest (seven starts), scoring twice, he moved on to Reggina in the summer of 1997.

❧ A MAN OF MANY AWARDS ❧

In addition to being the Premier League's highest-ever goalscorer with 260 career goals (112 with Blackburn Rovers and 148 with Newcastle United), Alan Shearer is Newcastle United's all-time leading goalscorer with 206 from 404 games (1996–97 to 2005–06). He also holds the Geordies' European goals record with 30 and was the leading goalscorer for his club for ten seasons: Blackburn Rovers 1994–95 and 1995–96, Newcastle United 1996–97, 1998–99, 1999–2000, 2001–02, 2002–03, 2003–04, 2004–05 and 2005–06. Alan was inducted into the English Football Hall of Fame in 2004 and is named in FIFA's list of the "100 Greatest Living Footballers". He was also named as the Overall Player of the Decade and the Domestic Player of the Decade when the Premier League held an awards ceremony to celebrate the first ten years of the Premiership (1992–93 to 2001–02).

❧ POMPEY'S 12TH MAN ❧

Portsmouth retired the No. 12 shirt in honour of their fans, their "12th man on the pitch".

⚜ SPURS PREMIER LEAGUE FANTASY XI ⚜

1
Brad
FRIEDEL

2
Stephen
CARR

6
Sol
CAMPBELL

5
Ledley
KING
(capt)

3
Justin
EDINBURGH

7
Aaron
LENNON

4
Jermaine
JENAS

8
Gareth
BALE

10
Jurgen
KLINSMANN

9
Teddy
SHERINGHAM

11
Jermain
DEFOE

Substitutes

Paul *ROBINSON* • Garr *MABBUTT* • Michael *DAWSON* • Gus *POYET* •
Darren *ANDERTON* • Dimitar *BERBATOV* • Robbie *KEANE*

Manager

Harry *REDKNAPP*

Did You Know That?

On December 26, 2007, Robbie Keane became only the 13th player
in the history of the league to score 100 Premiership goals

⚜ MANAGERIAL MUSICAL CHAIRS ⚜

In November 1994 Gerry Francis left Queen's Park Rangers and
became the new boss of Tottenham Hotspur. Ray Wilkins, who had
left Loftus Road in February 1995 to take up the position of player-
coach at Crystal Palace, returned to QPR as player-manager. Spurs
ended the season seventh in the Premiership with QPR just two
points and one place below them in eighth position.

⚜ THE CUNNING FOXES ⚜

In their first season in the Premiership, 1996–97, Martin O'Neill
guided Leicester City to an impressive ninth place, while the Foxes
also beat Middlesbrough in the 1997 League Cup final at Wembley.

✄ MARCH MADNESS FOR ERIC ✄

Manchester United's Eric Cantona became the first player to be sent off in consecutive Premier League games. On 19 March 1994, the enigmatic Frenchman was dismissed after stamping on Swindon Town's John Moncur during United's 2–2 draw at the County Ground. Three days later, Cantona was given an early bath at Highbury in United's 2–2 draw with the Gunners, although this decision was somewhat harsh. Despite his double whammy, Cantona scored 25 times for the champions over the course of the season, helped the Reds to the domestic Double and their second successive Premiership crown, and was voted the PFA Player of the Year.

✄ UNLUCKY 13 FOR RANGERS ✄

After enjoying 13 years among the big boys, Queen's Park Rangers lost their top-flight status in 1995–96 when they finished the season second from bottom of the Premiership. The loss of Les Ferdinand, sold to Newcastle United for £6 million, was one of the major factors for the London side's poor season.

✄ LE GOD RETIRES ✄

A terrible start to the 2001–02 season cost Southampton manager Stuart Gray the sack less than six months after he took charge at St Mary's. Gordon Strachan, who had left Coventry City, was appointed as Gray's successor and steered the Saints to an 11th-place finish in the table. It was the last season at Southampton for Matthew Le Tissier, nicknamed "Le God" by the Southampton fans, as he took the decision to hang up his boots after 16 years of loyal service to the Saints. However, Le Tissier was kept on by Strachan as a coach at St Mary's.

✄ JOB CUTS ON MERSEYSIDE ✄

In December 1993, Howard Kendall's second spell in charge of Everton ended when he resigned and walked out of Goodison Park. All was not well on the other side of Stanley Park either, and a month later Liverpool sacked Graeme Souness after losing at home to Bristol City in the third round of the FA Cup. Everton replaced Kendall with Norwich City boss Mike Walker, and their neighbours promoted coach Roy Evans to manager. John Deehan took over from Mike Walker at Carrow Road.

❧ OL' BLUE EYES IS BACK IN TOWN ❧

On 6 July 2007, Manchester City announced that Sven-Goran Eriksson had been appointed manager in place of Stuart Pearce. The former England coach guided City to wins in their opening three games, including a 1–0 win over Manchester United in the Manchester derby, to send City to the top of the Premier League.

❧ REDS CONTINUE HOT STREAK ❧

Manchester United finished runners-up to Arsenal in season 1997–98, which meant that since the Premier League began in 1992–93 the Red Devils had never finished below runners-up position (four wins, two second places). Meanwhile Arsenal became the third different team to win the Premiership title after United (1992–93, 1993–94, 1995–96 & 1996–97) and Blackburn Rovers (1994–95).

❧ AL PLAYS THE TOON ❧

At the end of the 1995–96 season Alan Shearer left Blackburn Rovers and signed for Newcastle United for what was then a world-record transfer fee of £15 million.

❧ KEEGAN TURNS BLUE ❧

When Manchester City sacked Joe Royle at the end of the 2000–01 season following the club's relegation to Division One, they brought in the former England manager Kevin Keegan to try and win promotion back into the Premier League. Keegan had resigned as the coach of England on 7 October 2000 shortly after his team lost 1–0 at home to Germany in their opening 2002 World Cup qualifying game.

❧ NAMED AND NUMBERED ❧

At the start of the 1993–94 season the Premier League introduced squad numbers for England's top-flight clubs.

❧ PREMIERSHIP TALK (11) ❧

"I would love an Aston Martin but if you ask me £1m for an Aston Martin, I tell you, you are crazy because they cost £250,000."
*Former Chelsea manager **Jose Mourinho***

ஜ FINAL PREMIERSHIP TABLE 1999–2000 ஜ

Pos	Team	P	W	D	L	F	A	Pts
1.	Manchester United (C)	38	28	7	3	97	45	91
2.	Arsenal	38	22	7	9	73	43	73
3.	Leeds United	38	21	6	11	58	43	69
4.	Liverpool	38	19	10	9	51	30	67
5.	Chelsea	38	18	11	9	53	34	65
6.	Aston Villa	38	15	13	10	46	35	58
7.	Sunderland	38	16	10	12	57	56	58
8.	Leicester City	38	16	7	15	55	55	55
9.	West Ham United	38	15	10	13	52	53	55
10.	Tottenham Hotspur	38	15	8	15	57	49	53
11.	Newcastle United	38	14	10	14	63	54	52
12.	Middlesbrough	38	14	10	14	46	52	52
13.	Everton	38	12	14	12	59	49	50
14.	Coventry City	38	12	8	18	47	54	44
15.	Southampton	38	12	8	18	45	62	44
16.	Derby County	38	9	11	18	44	57	38
17.	Bradford City	38	9	9	20	38	68	36
18.	Wimbledon (R)	38	7	12	19	46	74	33
19.	Sheffield Wednesday (R)	38	8	7	23	38	70	31
20.	Watford (R)	38	6	6	26	35	77	24

ஜ NO WAY PAST ஜ

When Tottenham Hotspur manager Andre Villas-Boas selected Hugo Lloris, his 2012 summer signing from Olympique Lyonnais, over Brad Friedel for Spurs' Premier League match against Aston Villa at White Hart Lane on 7 October 2012, it brought the veteran American goalkeeper's record run of 310 consecutive Premier League starts to an end. Then already 33, Friedel's run began on 1 August 2004 when he began the 2004-05 season as Blackburn Rovers' first-choice goalkeeper.

Chelsea's Petr Cech, set the standard for the most clean sheets in a season with 21 in 2004-05 Edwin Van der Sar matched the record in 2008–09, the season in which the Dutchman broke the world single-season record for minutes between goals conceded, 1,311. David James holds the record of having kept the most Premier League clean sheets in total with 173 playing for Liverpool, Aston Villa, West Ham United, Manchester City and Portsmouth. But England's former No.1 also holds the unwanted record of conceding the most goals, 665.

✂ THE PREMIERSHIP SIX ✂

There are six clubs which have played at least one season in the Premier League that do not share their last name with any of the other 92 clubs in the Premier League/Football League: Aston Villa, Crystal Palace, Nottingham Forest Queen's Park Rangers, Sheffield Wednesday.and Tottenham Hotspur There are 15 teams among the 92 (excluding AFC Wimbledon/Wimbledon), the others being: Accrington Stanley, AFC Bournemouth, Crewe Alexandra, Dagenham & Redbridge, Leyton Orient, MK Dons, Plymouth Argyle, Port Vale and Preston North End.

✂ STEPPING INTO THE LIGHT ✂

At the end of the 1995–96 season Peter Reid guided Sunderland to First Division championship glory and Premiership football in season 1996–97. Meanwhile Jim Smith helped Derby County win promotion to the Premiership and Martin O'Neill secured his third promotion in four seasons by taking Leicester City into the Premier League via the First Division play-offs.

✂ WE WANT OUR TROPHY BACK ✂

During the summer of 1998, after United finished runners-up to Arsenal in season 1997–98, Alex Ferguson raided Manchester United's coffers and broke the club's record transfer fee twice in his bid to put United back on top, where all their fans felt they belonged. To replace Gary Pallister, who had left the club, Fergie splashed out £10.75 million to secure the services of the 25-year-old Dutch centre-back Jaap Stam. Then he swooped for Aston Villa's Trinidad & Tobago international striker Dwight Yorke, for whom he paid £12.6 million. Fergie rounded off his summer spending with the £5m acquisition of the Swedish international winger Jesper Blomqvist from Parma. The spending worked as United won the Treble.

✂ ANELKA'S GOLDEN BOOT ... PART 1 ✂

Five years after finishing joint fourth in the Premier League goalscoring table with 17 goals for Arsenal in the 1998–99 season, Nicolas Anelka again finished joint fourth in season 2003–04, and again with 17 goals, but this time as a Manchester City player. Anelka was Manchester City's record purchase when Kevin Keegan signed him from Paris Saint-Germain in the summer of 2002 for £12 million.

⚜ CAT'S NINE LIVES ⚜

On 24 August 2007, Sunderland manager Roy Keane signed his former Manchester United team-mate Andy Cole. Sunderland was Cole's eighth Premiership club, following spells at Newcastle United, Manchester United, Blackburn Rovers, Fulham, Manchester City, Birmingham City and Portsmouth (while on loan from Birmingham). He actually began his career at Arsenal in pre-Premiership days and went out on loan to both Fulham and Bristol City, before making the move to Ashton Gate permanent.

⚜ UNITED BUST BANK TWICE ⚜

At the end of the 2000–01 season, champions Manchester United broke their own club record transfer fee twice. The first signing was the Dutch international striker Ruud van Nistelrooy, for whom United paid PSV Eindhoven a cool £19 million. This was followed by a whopping £28.1 million for Lazio's Argentine midfielder Juan Sebastian Veron. At the time Veron was the most expensive footballer in the history of British football.

⚜ WHEN FIFTH BECOMES FIRST ⚜

Despite Sir Alex Ferguson leading Manchester United to their third consecutive Premiership title in 2001, their seventh in nine years, the Manager of the Year Award went to Ipswich Town's George Burley. The Suffolk club finished fifth in the table, above clubs with far greater resources, including Chelsea (sixth), Aston Villa (eighth), Newcastle United (tenth), Tottenham Hotspur (11th) and Everton (16th).

⚜ BANGING THEM IN ⚜

Newcastle star striker Alan Shearer finished as the Premiership's top goalscorer in season 1996–97, with 25 goals in 31 games.

⚜ NO CHEER FOR SPARKY ⚜

On their way to securing their second domestic Double in 1995–96 Manchester United beat Chelsea 2–1 at Villa Park in the FA Cup semi-final. Mark "Sparky" Hughes was in the Chelsea team that lost to the rampant Red Devils. Ironically, he had scored for the Reds in their 4–0 FA Cup final win over the Blues in 1994 when United claimed their first Double success.

❧ ENGLAND PREMIER LEAGUE FANTASY XI ❧

1
David
SEAMAN
(ARSENAL & MAN CITY)

2
Gary
NEVILLE
(MANCHESTER UTD)

6
Tony
ADAMS
(ARSENAL, capt.)

5
Rio
FERDINAND
(WEST HAM, LEEDS & MAN UTD)

3
Stuart
PEARCE
(NOTTINGHAM FOR & WEST HAM)

7
David
BECKHAM
(MANCHESTER UTD)

4
Steven
GERRARD
(LIVERPOOL)

11
John
BARNES
(LIVERPOOL, NEWCASTLE & CHARLTON)

9
Michael
OWEN
(LIVERPOOL & NEWCASTLE)

10
Alan
SHEARER
(SOUTHAMPTON, BLACKBURN & NEWCASTLE)

8
Wayne
ROONEY
(EVERTON & MANCHESTER UTD)

Substitutes

Tim *FLOWERS (Southampton, Blackburn & Leicester)* • John *TERRY (Chelsea)*
Ashley *COLE (Arsenal & Chelsea)* • Frank *LAMPARD (West Ham & Chelsea)* •
Owen *HARGREAVES (Manchester Utd)* • Ian *WRIGHT (Arsenal & West Ham)* •
Peter *BEARDSLEY (Everton, Newcastle & Bolton)* •

Manager
Sir Bobby *ROBSON* CBE

Did You Know That?

Gary Neville is England's most-capped right-back, with 85. He only
scored once in an England shirt, an own goal versus Croatia.

❧ KEANE CENTURION ❧

Robbie Keane's 100th Tottenham Hotspur goal came in a 2–0 Premier
League defeat of Sunderland at White Hart Lane on 19 January 2008.

❧ AN IMPRESSIVE DEBUT ❧

Newcastle United, playing in their first season in the Premiership in
1993–94, finished third in the table behind champions Manchester
United and runners-up Blackburn Rovers. The Magpies were
spearheaded by their 22-year-old striker Andy Cole, who finished
the season as the league's top scorer with 34 goals from 40 games.

♆ FOREIGN IMPORTS ♆

The following table lists the Top 10 clubs which have played the most number of foreign players (those from outside of England, Scotland, Northern Ireland and Wales) in a Premier League game since the inaugural season in 1992–93 up to the end of 2012–13. This list includes only those players who made at least one appearance in the Premier League:

Rank	Club	No. of Foreign Players
1	Chelsea	104
2	Manchester City	96
3	Arsenal	94
4	Liverpool	91
5	West Ham United	89
6	Bolton Wanderers	88
=	Fulham	88
8	Newcastle United	80
=	Tottenham Hotspur	80
10	Blackburn Rovers	79

Did You Know That?
Manchester United, the Premier League's most successful club has relied far more on home-grown talent. The 13-times champions have fielded only 64 foreign players in Premier League matches.

♆ A NEW VILLAIN IN TOWN ♆

In February 1998, Brian Little left the managerial hot seat at Aston Villa and was replaced by Wycombe Wanderers' John Gregory. Gregory had previously been a coach at Villa Park, and after taking charge he guided the team to seventh place in the Premiership and automatic UEFA Cup qualification.

♆ THE TEESIDE HERO ♆

When Middlesbrough won the League Cup in 2003–04, Steve McClaren became the first English manager to win one of English football's three major prizes since Brian Little guided Aston Villa to League Cup success over Leeds United in 1996. McClaren was also the first man to take Middlesbrough into European competition, as they qualified for the 2004–05 UEFA Cup.

🔀 ALL CHANGE AT ANFIELD 🔀

After enjoying a good World Cup in the summer of 2002, Senegal player El Hadji Diouf was signed for Liverpool by manager Gerard Houllier. The arrival of the Senegalese international at Anfield signalled the end of Nicolas Anelka's loan stay at the club and he was sold to newly promoted Manchester City by his Turkish club Trabzonspor for £13 million. However, this was far from the end of the Reds' summer transfer dealings as Houllier then handed over £4.5 million for the French international winger Bruno Cheyrou, while Nick Barmby, Jari Litmanen and the long-serving Jamie Redknapp followed Anelka out of Anfield.

🔀 HUNG-UP OVER YOU 🔀

At the end of the 2005–06 season two of the Premiership's outstanding players, Dennis Bergkamp of Arsenal and Newcastle United's Alan Shearer, hung up their football boots for good. Shearer had hoped to play until the end of the campaign, but minutes after converting a penalty to give the Toon Army the lead against Sunderland at the Stadium of Light on 17 April 2006, he suffered a knee injury that brought his career to a premature close.

🔀 NO CHARITY FOR THE GEORDIES 🔀

On 11 August 1996, Manchester United faced Newcastle United in the traditional opener to the new football season, the FA Charity Shield at Wembley. Manchester United won the game 4–0.

🔀 STRIKER GOES ON STRIKE 🔀

Nottingham Forest's Pierre van Hooijdonk went on strike at the start of the 1998–99 season. Forest's leading goalscorer when they won the First Division championship the previous season was unhappy with the news that fellow strike-partner Kevin Campbell had been sold to Trabzonspor in Turkey for £2.5 million. During the 1997–98 season van Hooijdonk scored 34 times for Forest and Campbell found the net 24 times. The Dutch striker asked for a transfer, but it was refused, so he kept fit by training with one of his former clubs, NAC Breda in the Netherlands. He eventually returned to the City Ground in October 1998, but by then Forest where already in a relegation battle, sitting bottom of the Premiership without a win in nine league games, and eventually failed to beat the drop.

✷ TOOTHLESS UP FRONT ✷

Manchester City finished 16th in the Premiership table during the 1993–94 season and scored a miserable 38 goals, with their leading league goalscorer only finding the back of the net six times. It was their lowest finish in the top flight since suffering relegation from Division One at the end of the 1986–87 season. City were so poor up front that all three relegated clubs scored more goals than them, while only Ipswich Town scored fewer, with 35.

✷ BORING, BORING ARSENAL ✷

Although a total of 1,222 goals were scored in the inaugural FA Premier League season of 1992–93, Arsenal only accounted for 40 of them, the lowest goals tally of any of the 22 teams in the League. The Gunners, First Division champions in 1991, finished in tenth place.

✷ HAT-TRICK KINGS ✷

Alan Shearer has scored more Premiership hat-tricks than any other player in its 21-season history (1992–2013). Here is the top five:

	Player	Premier League clubs	Hat-tricks
1.	Alan Shearer	Blackburn, Newcastle	11
2.	Robbie Fowler	Liverpool, Leeds, Man City, Blackburn	9
3.	Thierry Henry	Arsenal	8
=	Michael Owen*	Liverpool, Newcastle, Man Utd, Stoke	8
5.	Wayne Rooney*	Everton, Manchester Utd	6

* Played in the Premier League in 2012–13

✷ MACCA AND GROWLER PARTNERSHIP ✷

Robbie Fowler and Steve McManaman have a horseracing business – "The Macca and Growler Partnership". They have several horses with trainer Martin Pipe.

✷ KENNY'S RUUD REPLACEMENT ✷

Shortly after the start of the 1998–99 Premiership season Newcastle United sacked manager Kenny Dalglish and replaced him with the former Chelsea player-coach Ruud Gullit.

⚜ OLD GUNS MAKE WAY FOR NEW GUNS ⚜

After helping Arsenal to the domestic Double in season 2001–02, Tony Adams, aged 35, and Lee Dixon, aged 38, retired. Adams had been at the club for 19 years, 14 of them as captain, while Dixon had been there for 14 years. Shortly after starting a Sports Science degree at Brunel University, Adams was appointed the manager of Wycombe Wanderers in November 2003, but he could not save them from relegation to League Two in season 2003–04. He resigned in November 2004 and, in July 2005, he took up a trainee coaching post with the Dutch side Feyenoord before moving to Portsmouth in June 2006 as assistant to manager Harry Redknapp. Following the departure of Adams, Arsene Wenger appointed Patrick Vieira as the new Arsenal captain for the 2002–03 season.

⚜ PROLIFIC AL ⚜

In season 1995–96 Blackburn Rovers, the defending Premiership Champions, could only manage a seventh-place finish in the Premiership table. Rovers scored 61 Premier League goals from their 38 games, and remarkably Alan Shearer scored 31 of them.

⚜ INTERWOVEN FATES ⚜

In November 2002 Sunderland sacked their manager Peter Reid and replaced him at the Stadium of Light with Howard Wilkinson. In March 2003 Reid was appointed the interim manager of Leeds United after they sacked Terry Venables – Wilkinson having been the manager of Leeds United from 1988 to 1996. Moreover, Venables was England manager from 1994 to 1996, and later Wilkinson managed the England team on a caretaker capacity in 1999 after Glenn Hoddle was sacked.

⚜ A LEAGUE OF NATIONS ⚜

In the 21-season history of the Premiership 1992–2013, more than 1,400 players from 96 countries have played at least one League match for one of the 45 clubs to compete in England's top flight.

⚜ WIGAN'S UNWANTED RECORD ⚜

In 2012–13, Wigan Athletic became the first team ever to win the FA Cup and suffer relegation from the top tier in the same season.

♟ ROY KEANE ♟

"Fail to prepare, prepare to fail" is a line from Roy's autobiography, simply entitled *Keane*, and this just about summed up Roy's playing career. Roy was a warrior on the pitch, who would lead from the front as he took the battle to the opposition. Outspoken by nature, he was a powerful, aggressive player who never shirked a tackle and a true midfield general, who was the driving force of Manchester United's midfield for 12 years from 1993 to 2005.

Roy Maurice Keane was born in Cork, Republic of Ireland, on 10 August 1971. In 1989 he signed as a semi-professional with Cobh Ramblers before joining Brian Clough's Nottingham Forest for £20,000. Few players can say that they played for two managerial legends, but Keano can. After Forest were relegated at the end of the 1993 season, Roy received overtures from a number of clubs. He chose Manchester United, the inaugural FA Premier League winners, and joined for a record transfer fee of £3.75 million. In his first season at Old Trafford, United won the Double, a feat they repeated in season 1995–96.

After United had clinched their fourth Premiership crown in five seasons in 1996–97, Keano was appointed the captain following the shock retirement of Eric Cantona. United's inspirational captain missed much of the 1997–98 season with a cruciate knee-ligament injury, but returned for the 1998–99 season and helped guide the side to the unprecedented Treble, although he missed the dramatic Champions League final win over Bayern Munich through suspension. In 2000 Keano was voted the PFA Players' Player of the Year.

Roy captained Manchester United to nine major honours, making him the Red Devils' most successful captain of all time. During his time at Old Trafford, United won seven league titles, four FA Cups, the UEFA Champions League and the Intercontinental Cup. In January 2006 Keano left United and joined Celtic, where he won the Scottish Premier League and Scottish League Cup, before hanging up his boots in May 2006.

In August 2006, the lure of management took him to Sunderland's Stadium of Light where he was reunited with his former international team-mate Niall Quinn, the club's chairman. In his first season as a manager he guided the Black Cats to the Championship title and promotion back to the Premier League. He left the Black Cats in December 2008 and spent two years in charge of Ipswich Town. Roy is now a regular analyst on television, unafraid as ever to speak his mind.

Did You Know That?
At international level, Keano won 66 caps for the Republic of Ireland.

♊ PREMIERSHIP TALK (12) ♋

"You see how Spanish, Italians, Portuguese play football. I don't say they are perfect, I say English football has a few things to learn from them in the same way they have a lot of things to learn from English football."
Chelsea manager Jose Mourinho

♊ 100 PREMIER LEAGUE GOALS CLUB ♋

At the end of the 2012–13 season, 23 players had scored at least 100 Premier League goals. Fifteen had passed the 120 goals mark, but only nine managed more than 130: They were:

261	Alan Shearer	Blackburn, Newcastle
188	Andrew Cole	Newcastle, Manchester United, Blackburn, Fulham, Manchester City, Portsmouth
176	Thierry Henry	Arsenal
165	Frank Lampard	West Ham, Chelsea
163	Robbie Fowler	Liverpool, Leeds, Manchester City
156	Wayne Rooney	Everton, Manchester United
150	Michael Owen	Liverpool, Newcastle, Manchester United, Stoke
149	Les Ferdinand	QPR, Newcastle, Tottenham Hotspur, West Ham, Leicester, Bolton
147	Teddy Sheringham	Nottingham Forest, Tottenham Hotspur, Manchester United, Portsmouth, West Ham

Did You Know That?
Only five players scored all their 100 goals for one club: Henry (above), Ryan Giggs (Manchester Utd, 109), Paul Scholes (Manchester Utd, 107), Matt Le Tissier (Southampton, 101) and Didier Drogba (Chelsea, 100).

♊ GEORDIES' RECORD START ♋

In 1994–95 Newcastle United made their best ever top-flight start, winning their first six games. They ended the season in sixth place.

♊ SAINTS MOVE TO ST MARY'S ♋

The 2000–01 season was Southampton's last season at The Dell and after 103 years the Saints moved to their new all-seater stadium at St Mary's. With a 32,000 capacity, St Mary's contained more than twice the number of seats than The Dell.

✄ FINAL PREMIERSHIP TABLE 2000–2001 ✄

Pos	Team	P	W	D	L	F	A	Pts
1.	Manchester United (C)	38	24	8	6	79	31	80
2.	Arsenal	38	20	10	8	63	38	70
3.	Liverpool	38	20	9	9	71	39	69
4.	Leeds United	38	20	8	10	64	43	68
5.	Ipswich Town	38	20	6	12	57	42	66
6.	Chelsea	38	17	10	11	68	45	61
7.	Sunderland	38	15	12	11	46	41	57
8.	Aston Villa	38	13	15	10	46	43	54
9.	Charlton Athletic	38	14	10	14	50	57	52
10.	Southampton	38	14	10	14	40	48	52
11.	Newcastle United	38	14	9	15	44	50	51
12.	Tottenham Hotspur	38	13	10	15	47	54	49
13.	Leicester City	38	14	6	18	39	51	48
14.	Middlesbrough	38	9	15	14	44	44	42
15.	West Ham United	38	10	12	16	45	50	42
16.	Everton	38	11	9	18	45	59	42
17.	Derby County	38	10	12	16	37	59	42
18.	Manchester City (R)	38	8	10	20	41	65	34
19.	Coventry City (R)	38	8	10	20	36	63	34
20.	Bradford City (R)	38	5	11	22	30	70	26

✄ FERGIE THE PEACEMAKER ✄

On 15th February 2008, Eamonn Holmes had Prime Minister Gordon Brown as a guest on his BBC Radio 5 show. Mr Brown confessed to being a Raith Rovers fan but said he also liked Tottenham Hotspur and Manchester United. Indeed, the PM went as far as to suggest that Sir Alex Ferguson could help to bring peace to the Middle East: "Prime Minister Olmert of Israel and Mr Fayyad, Prime Minister of the Palestinian Authority, are both United supporters. We had a plan at one stage that I would take them both to a match. I have found, to my great surprise, that sport is actually a means by which people work and communicate," said Mr Brown.

✄ MOVING SOUTH ✄

On 27 November 2007, Alex McLeish resigned as manager of Scotland's national side. The following day he was unveiled by Birmingham City as Steve Bruce's successor. Bruce had quit the Blues on 19 November 2007 to take charge of Wigan Athletic.

❧ SEASON OF CHANGE IN THE HOT SEATS ❧

Only four Premiership clubs entered June 2013 with the same manager as had been in charge in May 2012: Arsene Wenger (Arsenal), Martin Jol (Fulham), Alan Pardew (Newcastle United) and Sam Allardyce (West Ham United). The biggest names to leave their clubs soon after the end of the 2011–12 season were: Roy Hodgson, who left West Bromwich Albion to become England coach and Kenny Dalglish, who was sacked by Liverpool and replaced by Swansea manager Brendon Rogers. In November, Chelsea sacked Roberto Di Matteo, six months and two days after their UEFA Champions League triumph. But they faded into insignificance in mid May 2013, when Sir Alex Ferguson announced his retirement. His replacement was unveiled two days later – David Moyes, who moved from Everton. Four days later, on the first anniversary of winning their first Premiership championship for 44 years and two days after a shock FA Cup final defeat against Wigan, Manchester City relieved Roberto Mancini of his duties.

❧ AN UNHAPPY ENDING ❧

In their final home game of the 2002–03 season Manchester City lost to Southampton in the Premier League. It was the Citizens' last ever game at Maine Road before moving to Eastlands (aka the City of Manchester Stadium, venue for the 2002 Commonwealth Games).

❧ THE KOP'S LAST STAND ❧

"The Kop's Last Stand" was the name given to Liverpool's match programme for the visit of Norwich City to Anfield on 30 April 1994 in the Premiership. It marked the last-ever game in front of a standing Kop, and before the match a tearful Gerry Marsden performed the Liverpool anthem "You'll Never Walk Alone". However, many Liverpool fans among the crowd of 44,339 will want to forget the game itself since Norwich City spoiled the party, winning 1–0 thanks to a goal from Jeremy Goss – in front of the Kop!

❧ WHEN THE WELL WENT DRY ❧

When Manchester City lost their final home game 1–0 to Manchester United on 5 May 2007, they set a new record for the fewest goals scored at home in a season by a club in the top flight, a meagre ten. City had not scored at home since New Year's Day 2007.

⚜ THE COSTLY LADS ⚜

The top 10 announced transfer fees involving a Premier League club since the start of the inaugural season in 1992 to the end of the January 2013 window are below Carlos Tevez's move across Manchester, from United to City in 2009, was for an undisclosed fee.

Pos	Player	From	To	Date	Fee
1.	Fernando Torres	Liverpool	Chelsea	January 2011	50m
2.	Sergio Aguero	Atl Madrid	Man City	July 2011	38m
3.	Andy Carroll	Newcastle	Liverpool	January 2011	35m
4.	Robinho	Real Madrid	Man City	September 2008	32.5m
5.	Andrei Shevchenko	AC Milan	Chelsea	May 2006	30.m
6.	Dimitar Berbatov	Spurs	Man Utd	September 2008	30.75m
7.	Rio Ferdinand	Leeds	Man Utd	July 2002	29.1m
8.	Juan Veron	Lazio	Man Utd	July 2001	28.1m
9.	Edin Dzeko	Wolfsburg	Man City	January 2011	27m
10.	Wayne Rooney	Everton	Man Utd	August 2006	25.6m

⚜ PREMIER LEAGUE'S EUROPEAN TRIO ⚜

At the end of the 1998–99 season UEFA increased the Premiership's UEFA Champions League places for the 1999–2000 season to three. Manchester United qualified as Premiership champions and Arsenal as runners-up, while Chelsea grabbed the final qualifying place by coming third. Meanwhile fourth-placed Leeds United qualified for the UEFA Cup, and fifth-placed West Ham United also gained a UEFA Cup place via the Intertoto Cup route. Tottenham Hotspur, League Cup winners, and Newcastle United, FA Cup runners-up, also claimed UEFA Cup slots.

⚜ THREE BOSSES, ONE RELEGATION ⚜

In October 2001 Jim Smith rejected Derby County's offer of a position as director of football and resigned as manager. Smith was replaced as manager by Colin Todd, who had won First Division championship-winners' medals as a player with Derby County in 1972 and 1975. However, Todd only lasted 18 games in charge before being sacked following an embarrassing FA Cup third-round exit to Division Three side Bristol Rovers. He was replaced by John Gregory, who had been sacked as manager of Aston Villa less than a week earlier. However, the Rams ended the season one place off the foot of the Premiership table and were relegated to Division One.

ᚠ TIGHT GUNNERS ᚠ

Despite conceding 20 fewer Premiership goals (17 to 37) than Manchester United in the 1998–99 season, Arsenal were still pipped to the Premier League title thanks to United's awesome firepower. With their strike force of Andy Cole, Teddy Sheringham, Ole Gunnar Solskjaer and Dwight Yorke, United scored 21 more Premiership goals than their title challengers (80 to 59).

ᚠ OFF WITHOUT A TOUCH ᚠ

Andreas Johansson and Keith Gillespie are joint holders of the unenviable Premiership record for the fewest touches of a ball in a game before being sent off. On 7 May 2006, Johansson came on as a substitute for Wigan Athletic against Arsenal and was quickly sent off, and Gillespie came on as a substitute for Sheffield United against Reading on 20 January 2007 and was also sent for a very early bath. Neither player touched the ball.

ᚠ WHO ATE ALL THE PIES? ᚠ

On the opening day of the 1993–94 season Coventry City visited Arsenal, the reigning FA Cup and League Cup holders, and came away with a 3–0 win courtesy of a hat-trick from Micky Quinn. During his two years with Coventry City (1992–94), Micky Quinn was nicknamed "Sumo" and was once famously hailed as the Premiership's "fastest player over a yard". In 2003, Quinn released his autobiography entitled *Who Ate All the Pies?*

ᚠ UNITED – A CLOSED BOOK ᚠ

By Christmas 2000 Manchester United were so far ahead of the chasing pack in the Premiership that the bookmakers closed their books on anyone catching them. United streaked to the title ten points clear of the Gunners and 11 in front of third-placed Liverpool.

ᚠ GAZZA THE DERBY KING ᚠ

Paul Gascoigne is the only player to have played in Tyne–Tees, Tees–Wear, Tyne–Wear, North London, Merseyside, Old Firm and Rome derbies. Gazza played for Newcastle United, Tottenham Hotspur, Middlesbrough, Everton, Glasgow Rangers and Lazio.

❧ PREMIERSHIP TALK (13) ❧

"I may be French, but I'm playing for Arsenal."
Thierry Henry (Arsenal)

❧ TOON IN TURMOIL ❧

When Kevin Keegan resigned as manager of Newcastle United in September 2008, it set off a calamitous chain of events. Chris Hughton was named caretaker manager for a few weeks until ex-Wimbledon boss Joe Kinnear became interim manager on a rolling monthly contract. Kinnear's deal was extended until the end of the season when, in February, he had another heart scare and had to step aside. Hughton was again briefly caretaker-boss until, embroiled in a relegation battle, Toon legend Alan Shearer was appointed for the final eight games of the campaign. The Premier League's all-time leading goalscorer enjoyed only one win in charge and Newcastle were relegated.

❧ MERSEYSIDE ESCAPOLOGISTS ❧

Everton only managed to avoid the drop into Division One at the end of the 1997–98 Premiership season on the final day on goal difference at the expense of Bolton Wanderers.

❧ A GREAT ESCAPE IN LONDON ❧

Following a number of defeats in January and February 2003, Leeds United were deep in a Premiership relegation battle. Having sacked David O'Leary the previous summer, the Leeds board then sacked his successor Terry Venables and replaced him with ex-Sunderland manager Peter Reid. In their penultimate game of the season, Leeds faced a daunting trip to London to play the reigning Premiership champions, Arsenal, themselves involved in a tense battle for the title with Manchester United. Remarkably, Leeds beat Arsenal 3–2 at Highbury, a result that ensured their Premiership survival – the result also handed Manchester United the Premiership crown.

❧ DOUBLE ROBBIE ❧

At the end of the 1995–96 season Liverpool's Robbie Fowler won the PFA Young Player of the Year award for the second year in succession. In January 1996 he also became the first player to win the Premier League Player of the Month Award in successive months.

❧ HEY, BIG SPENDERS ❧

When Fulham signed Danny Murphy from Spurs on the last day of the transfer window, 31 August 2007, they set a new Premier League record for the highest number of summer signings, 15.

❧ A DOUBLE LEGEND SWOOP ❧

At the end of the 1994–95 season, Glenn Hoddle, Chelsea's player-manager, hung up his football boots for good to concentrate on managing the Blues. Amazingly, Hoddle managed to persuade Manchester United's Mark Hughes and AC Milan's Ruud Gullit to join his Stamford Bridge revolution.

❧ EX-MEMBERS' UNIQUE TREBLE ❧

Charlton Athletic made a return to the Premiership tt the end of the 1999–2000 season by winning the First Division title. Manchester City finished runners-up to Charlton and were also promoted along with Ipswich Town, the First Division play-off winners. It was the first time in the eight-year history of the Premier League that the three teams promoted from the First Division were all former Premier League clubs.

❧ UNFIT FOR PREMIER LEAGUE SURVIVAL ❧

Middlesbrough had a rollercoaster season in 1996–97. They lost both domestic cup finals and were relegated from the Premiership in 19th place. However, Boro would have escaped relegation if they had not been docked three points by the Premier League as a punishment for postponing a league game against Blackburn Rovers in January 1997, just 24 hours before the game. The FA's assistant chief executive originally gave Boro permission to postpone the game, only for the FA to decide that the game should proceed after all. If Boro had played the game and replaced their first-team players with reserves and youth teamers they would have stayed up. The three points they lost would have secured 16th place in the Premiership and sent Coventry City down. Indeed, if they had won the game when it was played in May 1997 – they drew 0–0 – they would have survived. Boro's chairman Steve Gibson lodged an appeal with the Premier League at the time of the points deduction, claiming that the club simply did not have enough fit players to field a team, but the appeal was unsuccessful.

♊ BRITISH FOOTBALL'S RICH LIST ♊

Exact figures are not always revealed but the following Premier League stars reportedly had the biggest weekly salaries in 2012–13:

Highest earning Premier League players

1.	Eden Hazard	Chelsea	£185,000
2.	Wayne Rooney	Manchester Utd	£180,000
=	Robin van Persie	Manchester Utd	£180,000
=	Yaya Touré	Manchester City	£180,000
=	Carlos Tevez	Manchester City	£180,000
6.	Fernando Torres	Chelsea	£175,000
=	John Terry	Chelsea	£175,000
8.	David Silva	Manchester City	£160,000
9.	Samir Nasri	Manchester City	£140,000
=	Frank Lampard	Chelsea	£140,000

But the players' wages and wealth pale into insignificance against the value of the Premier League's wealthiest owners and benefactors:

Ten Richest Men in British Football

1.	Sheikh Mansour bin Zayed	Manchester City	£20.0bn
2.	Alisher Usmanov	Arsenal	£12.5bn
3.	Lakshmi Mittal	Queens Park Rangers	£12.0bn
4.	Roman Abramovich	Chelsea	£10.5bn
5.	The Liebherr Family	Southampton	£3.0bn
6.	Joe Lewis	Tottenham Hotspur	£2.8bn
7.	Stanley Kroenke	Arsenal	£1.8bn
8.	Malcolm Glazer & Family	Manchester United	£1.6bn
9.	Mike Ashley	Newcastle United	£1.4bn
10.	Mohamed Al-Fayed	Fulham	£1.3bn

♊ 15,000 VOLZ ♊

On 30 December 2006, Moritz Volz of Fulham scored the 15,000th FA Premier League goal in his side's 2–2 draw away to Chelsea. Barclaycard, the League's sponsor, gave £15,000 to the Fulham Community Sports Trust in Volz's name. Meanwhile, a fan who correctly predicted that the German would score the historic goal, in a contest organized by the Premier League, had the honour of presenting Volz with a special award prior to Fulham's home game versus Watford at Craven Cottage on New Year's Day 2007. After netting the historic goal, Fulham fans nicknamed him "15,000 Volz".

❧ THE SHERIFF OF NOTTINGHAM ❧

In October 1998, Nottingham Forest sacked manager Dave Bassett and replaced him with Ron Atkinson until the end of the 1998–99 season. In Big Ron's first game in charge of Forest, a home game against Arsenal, he famously walked into the opposition's dugout and sat down. When asked about it after the match, he waved the incident off in true Big Ron fashion. "For a moment I thought we had Bergkamp on our bench," said the new Forest boss. Unfortunately Atkinson could not save Forest from the drop into Division One at the end of the 1998–99 season, when they finished bottom of the table. In his 16 games in charge at the City Ground Big Ron won four, drew two and lost ten. After Forest's relegation Atkinson retired and David Platt, the former England captain, was brought to the club as player-manager.

❧ MILLENNIUM TOPPERS ❧

On New Year's Day 2000 Leeds United entered the new millennium sitting on top of the Premiership table. However, David O'Leary's side eventually finished the 1999–2000 season in third place – a yawning 22 points behind the runaway champions Manchester United.

❧ THE DYNAMIC DUO ❧

Andy Cole (34 goals) and Peter Beardsley (25 goals) scored 59 goals for Newcastle United in their 1993–94 Premiership campaign and both made the top three of the goalscoring charts for the season. The rest of the team only managed 23 between them while the Geordies, managed by their former player Kevin Keegan in their first season back in the top flight, finished third in the table and qualified for the UEFA Cup. Not surprisingly, Andy Cole won the 1993–94 PFA Young Player of the Year Award.

❧ FROM DUGOUT TO DESK JOB ❧

On 28 January 2008, Dennis Wise resigned as manager of Leeds United to take up his new role as director of football development at Newcastle United. Fans at both clubs were left stunned by Wise's move, which came less than a fortnight after Kevin Keegan had made a hero's return to St James' Park, succeeding Sam Allardyce as boss of the Magpies. Wise left with Leeds sitting in fifth place in League One, despite the club starting the season with a 15-point deduction.

♜ HISPANIC PREMIER LEAGUE FANTASY XI ♜

1
Jose Manuel
REINA
(SPAIN)

2 | **4** | **5** | **3**
Pablo | Ricardo | Fabriccio | Jose
ZABALETA | **CARVALHO** | **COLLOCINI** | **ENRIQUE**
(ARGENTINA) | *(PORTUGAL)* | *(ARGENTINA)* | *(SPAIN)*

7 | **6** | **8**
Cristiano | David | Cesc
RONALDO | **SILVA** | **FABREGAS**
(PORTUGAL) | *(ARGENTINA)* | *(SPAIN, CAPTAIN)*

9 | **10** | **11**
Fernando | Carlos | Sergio
TORRES | **TEVEZ** | **AGUERO**
(SPAIN) | *(ARGENTINA)* | *(ARGENTINA)*

Substitutes

Manuel **ALMUNIA** (Spain) • Paulo **FERREIRA** (Portugal) • Gilberto **SILVA** (Brazil) •
JUNINHO (Brazil) • Juan **MATA** (Spain) • **NANI** (Portugal) • Luis **SUAREZ** (Uruguay)

Manager

Jose **MOURINHO** (Portugal)

Did You Know That?

Cristiano Ronaldo's reputed €28.5 million overall earnings in 2012–13 made him the third-highest in world football, behind only Lionel Messi (€31.5 million) and David Beckham (€30.8 million).

♜ LANDLORDS RELEGATED ♜

In the inaugural Premiership season in 1992–93, Crystal Palace and Wimbledon both played their home games at Selhurst Park, London. At the end of the season landlords Palace were relegated while tenants Dons, finished a respectable 12th in the table.

♜ POPE SUPPORTS LIVERPOOL ♜

In 2004 Pope John Paul II granted an audience with players from the Polish national football team. During the audience in the Vatican, the Pontiff – who was born in Poland and was a goalkeeper in his youth – told Liverpool No.1 Jerzy Dudek that he was a keen supporter of the Reds and listened out for their results whenever they were playing.

❧ EURO MISERY FOR SPURS AND EVERTON ❧

Fourth-placed Tottenham and Everton (seventh) earned city bragging rights, over Chelsea (sixth) and Liverpool (eighth) in 2011–12. But they both missed out on their European dreams as the Blues and Reds took their places in the 2012–13 UEFA Champions League and UEFA Europa League, respectively. Chelsea, as UEFA Champions League winners, gained an automatic right to defend the trophy, thus sending Tottenham into the Europa League. The other two Europa League spots went to Newcastle – fifth in the Premiership – and Liverpool, winners of the 2012 Carling Cup, so Everton missed out altogether..

❧ ROVERS SKIPPING AGAIN ❧

In season 1997–98 Roy Hodgson guided Blackburn Rovers to sixth place in the Premiership and UEFA Cup football the following season. Chris Sutton ended the season as the Premiership's joint top goalscorer (18 goals) which was good enough to earn him a call-up to the England team. Sutton played in England's 2–0 friendly win over Cameroon at Wembley on 15 November 1997, his first and last cap for his country.

❧ SPARKY OF THE ROVERS ❧

In 2001–02 Blackburn Rovers lay third from bottom of the Premier League table when they faced Tottenham Hotspur in the Worthington (League) Cup final at the Millennium Stadium in Cardiff. However, the 1995 Premiership champions beat Spurs 2–1 to win the cup, and a good run of form then enabled Graeme Souness's side to climb away from the relegation zone and end the campaign tenth in the table. This winners medal was the last one won by striker Mark Hughes, who retired at the end of the 2001–02 season. Hughes, nicknamed Sparky, had an illustrious career that saw him capped 72 times by Wales, as well as playing for Manchester United (two spells), Barcelona, Bayern Munich (on loan), Chelsea, Southampton and Everton. With United, Sparky won three FA Cups (1985, 1990 and 1994), two Premier League titles (1993 and 1994), the League Cup (1992), the European Cup Winners' Cup (1991) and the European Super Cup (1991). During his time at Chelsea he added to his medal collection with a fourth FA Cup (1997), a second League Cup (1998) and a second European Cup Winners' Cup (1998). Hughes also managed the Wales national team and Blackburn, Manchester City, Fulham and Queens Park Rangers in the Premier League.

♘ FINAL PREMIERSHIP TABLE 2001–2002 ♘

Pos	Team	P	W	D	L	F	A	Pts
1.	Arsenal (C)	38	26	9	3	79	36	87
2.	Liverpool	38	24	8	6	67	30	80
3.	Manchester United	38	24	5	9	87	45	77
4.	Newcastle United	38	21	8	9	74	52	71
5.	Leeds United	38	18	12	8	53	37	66
6.	Chelsea	38	17	13	8	66	38	64
7.	West Ham United	38	15	8	15	48	57	53
8.	Aston Villa	38	12	14	12	46	47	50
9.	Tottenham Hotspur	38	14	8	16	49	53	50
10.	Blackburn Rovers	38	12	10	16	55	51	46
11.	Southampton	38	12	9	17	46	54	45
12.	Middlesbrough	38	12	9	17	35	47	45
13.	Fulham	38	10	14	14	36	44	44
14.	Charlton Athletic	38	10	14	14	38	49	44
15.	Everton	38	11	10	17	45	57	43
16.	Bolton Wanderers	38	9	13	16	44	62	40
17.	Sunderland	38	10	10	18	29	51	40
18.	Ipswich Town (R)	38	9	9	20	41	64	36
19.	Derby County (R)	38	8	6	24	33	63	30
20.	Leicester City (R)	38	5	13	20	30	64	28

♘ ARSENAL, LONDON'S FIFTH BEST CLUB ♘

In 1994–95, Arsenal, First Division winners in 1988–89 and 1990–91, finished 12th in the Premiership, and fifth among London's seven clubs. Above Arsenal were: Chelsea (11th), Wimbledon (ninth), Queen's Park Rangers (eighth), and Tottenham Hotspur (seventh). West Ham United were (14th) and Crystal Palace (19th).

♘ NEW BOYS HOLD THEIR OWN ♘

In 2011–12, for only the second time in the Premier League era, all three promoted teams avoided relegation. Swansea City finished 11th, Norwich City 12th and Queens Park Rangers 17th. In 2001–02 Blackburn Rovers, Bolton Wanderers and Fulham dodged the drop.

♘ CLOSEST EVER FINISH ♘

Manchester City's 2011–12 Premiership title was the first won on goal difference. Their +64 was eight better than neighbours United's +56.

☙ PREMIERSHIP TALK (14) ❧

"I prefer to play and lose rather than win, because I know in advance I'm going to win."
Eric Cantona (Manchester United)

☙ ELLAND ROAD MERRY-GO-ROUND ❧

In November 2003, Leeds United sacked their manager Peter Reid and appointed the club's first-team coach Eddie Gray as interim manager until the end of the 2003–04 season. When Gray, a Leeds United star of the 1970s, failed to save the Yorkshire club from relegation to the Championship, he was also sacked and replaced by his assistant Kevin Blackwell.

☙ BACK-TO-BACK DOUBLE FOR UNITED ❧

In season 1996–97, Manchester United won their second consecutive Premiership title and their fourth Championship in five seasons. It was also the second time the Red Devils achieved back-to-back Premier League titles, having previously won a second successive title in 1993–94. It was far from plain sailing, however – in October they lost three games and conceded 13 goals.

☙ FIRST OF THE MILLENNIUM ❧

The 1999–2000 season was the eighth of the Premier League, which was won by Manchester United, the reigning champions from 1998–99, as they claimed their sixth Premiership crown. Whereas the previous season Arsenal took the contest for the title right down to the wire – the Red Devils eventually pipped the Gunners by a single point – this time United romped away with the title, streets ahead of the opposition, winning the crown by a mammoth 18 points.

☙ THE NEW FACES ❧

Newcastle United (1993 Division One champions), West Ham United (1993 Division One runners-up) and Swindon Town (1993 Division One play-off final winners) all embarked on their first Premiership campaigns in season 1993–94. Only Swindon Town had never played in English football's top flight before: the Robins won the old Second Division play-off final in 1990, but were not allowed to take up their place in Division One because of financial irregularities.

℘ SPECIAL ONE DROPS BLUE BOMBSHELL ℘

Jose Mourinho sent shockwaves around the world of football when he left Chelsea by mutual consent on 20 September 2007, two days after their disappointing 1–1 home draw with Rosenborg in the UEFA Champions League and three days before their Premiership game against Manchester United at Old Trafford. The 44-year-old Portuguese manager arrived at Stamford Bridge in 2004 and won the Premier League title in his first two seasons in charge as well as the League Cup in 2005. In May 2007, he guided the Blues to FA Cup success and still had three years left on his contract, worth reputedly around £5 million a year. He took charge of Chelsea 185 times, winning 124 matches, drawing 40 and losing 21 – a record that also included a 60-match unbeaten home run in Premier League games.

℘ FOXES SIT ON TOP OF THE MOUNTAIN ℘

At the beginning of October 2000 Leicester City, under new manager Peter Taylor, sat proudly at the summit of the Premier League table. It was the first time since 1963 that Leicester City had reached such a dizzy height, and it only lasted two weeks, after which Manchester United assumed top spot and stayed there until the end of the season. Many Foxes fans thought that their club would struggle following Martin O'Neill's departure to manage Glasgow Celtic five months earlier, but Taylor ensured Premiership survival for Leicester City with a 13th-place finish in the table. However, it was the club's lowest finish since winning promotion to the Premiership in season 1995–96. In their last ten Premiership games of the season the Foxes suffered nine defeats and managed just one win. They never fully recovered from their shock home FA Cup exit to Second Division side Wycombe Wanderers.

℘ NOT SO SWEET SUGAR ℘

Tottenham Hotspur finished eighth at the end of the inaugural Premiership campaign in 1992–93, but chairman Alan Sugar sacked their chief executive, the highly popular Terry Venables, and his two head coaches Ray Clemence and Doug Livermore. Sugar helped curb the anger of the Spurs fans by appointing former hero Osvaldo Ardiles as the new man in charge at White Hart Lane. Ossie left West Bromwich Albion to take up the offer. Sugar's falling-out with Venables led to a High Court action, which Sugar won.

❧ LUCKY 13 FOR THE GEORDIES ❧

Despite only managing to finish in 13th place in the 1998–99 Premier League season, Newcastle United qualified for the 1999–2000 UEFA Cup competition because they lost in the final of the FA Cup (the European Cup Winners' Cup was contested for the last time in 1998–99). They lost to league champions Manchester United, who thus completed the coveted domestic Double (and subsequent Treble).

❧ LONDON'S BIG SPENDERS ❧

Chelsea were able to spend heavily going into the 2003–04 season thanks to their new owner Roman Abramovich's extensive bankroll. Some £100 million was spent by Claudio Ranieri to strengthen his side and push for the Premiership title. In the end, though, Chelsea could only manage to finish runners-up to Arsenal.

❧ THOUSANDTH LIVE GAME ❧

The 1–1 draw between Tottenham Hotspur and Blackburn Rovers at White Hart Lane on 10 May 2007 was the 1,000th live game to be shown by Sky Sports.

❧ A LONG WAY TO FALL … AND RISE ❧

Portsmouth suffered relegation from the Premier League in 2010 and suffered further relegations in both 2012 and 2013. They are the fourth team to go from the Premier League to the fourth tier, following Bradford City, Swindon Town and MK Dons (transplanted from Wimbledon). It does work both ways as 2013–14 Premiership clubs Hull City, Swansea City and Cardiff City have all gone in the other direction.

❧ THE DERBY KING ❧

Over the summer of 2001 Tottenham Hotspur purchased the German international Christian Ziege from Liverpool. Ziege had only been at Liverpool for a season and spent one season at Middlesbrough in 1999–2000. The stylish defender/midfielder began his career with Bayern Munich (1990–97) before joining AC Milan (1997–99). He is the only player to have played in the Munich, Milan, Tyne-Tees, Merseyside and London derby matches. Ziege won the UEFA Cup with Bayern Munich in 1996 and again with Liverpool in 2001.

♚ JOSE MOURINHO ♚

Jose Mario dos Santos Felix Mourinho was born in Setubal, Portugal, on 26 January 1963. His father, Felix, was a former goalkeeper and football manager. At college Mourinho obtained a degree in physical education, specializing in sports methodology. He joined Vila do Conde, where Felix was the head coach. After completing a UEFA coaching course, Jose coached in a high school but couldn't make a career as a footballer.

He was then given a backroom post at Estrela da Amadora before joining Vitoria Setubal's coaching staff. When former England manager Bobby Robson was appointed manager of Sporting Lisbon in 1993 he brought in Mourinho as his translator, and he took him with him when he moved to Porto in 1994. When Robson moved to Spain in 1996 to manage Barcelona, he again took Mourinho with him, but when Robson was fired in 1997, Mourinho stayed at the Nou Camp. Luis van Gaal, the new manager, actively involved Jose in team discussions and tactics before eventually allowing him to manage the Barcelona "B" team. In September 2000 his big chance came when he took up the manager's post at Benfica, but Jose resigned after only nine games following a row with the board. A successful year at Uniao de Leiria from January 2001 attracted the interest of FC Porto, who installed him as their new manager in January 2002 and he quickly brought success to the club, winning two Portuguese championships (2003 and 2004), the Portuguese Cup (2003), the UEFA Cup (2003) and the UEFA Champions League (2004).

All of Europe now wanted Mourinho, but it was Chelsea, bankrolled by the Russian billionaire Roman Abramovich, who secured the services of the "Special One". When Jose walked through the gates of Stamford Bridge, Chelsea had not won the First Division title in 49 years, but he corrected that in his first season in charge (2004–05), having already won the Carling Cup three months earlier. Chelsea retained the Premiership title the following season and 2006–07 lifted both domestic Cups. On 20 September 2007, Mourinho lleft Chelsea by "mutual consent".

A move to Italy and Internazionale of Milan resulted in a second UEFA Champions League success before Jose went to Spain and won the La Liga title with Real Madrid and was the only coach in the country with a winning regcord against the all-conquering Barcelona. In 2013, after Real had finished runners-up behind Barça and lost in the Champions League semi-final, he left Madrid to return to Chelsea.

Did You Know That?
Jose Mourinho threw his trademark overcoat and Premier League winners medal into the Stamford Bridge stands in 2006.

❧ THE KING OF HAT-TRICK KINGS ❧

During the summer of 2004, West Bromwich Albion paid Cardiff City £3 million for the services of their Zambian-born Welsh international striker Robert Earnshaw. When Earnshaw scored a hat-trick for the Baggies in their Premiership win over Charlton Athletic on 19 March 2005, the Welsh striker became the first player to have bagged a hat-trick in all four levels of English professional league football (Premier League, Championship, League Divisions One and Two), in the FA Cup and League Cup and at international level.

❧ THE WHITE FEATHER ❧

Despite scoring 31 goals in all competitions for Middlesbrough in 1996–97, Fabrizio Ravanelli, nicknamed the "White Feather", could not save the club from relegation from the Premiership.

❧ MR BO JANGLES ❧

In February 1995, Coventry City sacked their manager Phil Neal and replaced him with Ron Atkinson, nicknamed "Big Ron" and "Mr Bo Jangles", who himself had been sacked by Aston Villa three months earlier. Atkinson moved quickly to bring in 37-year-old Gordon Strachan from Leeds United as his assistant manager, a move that paid off as the Sky Blues managed to avoid the drop, finishing 16th in the table.

❧ IN IT FOR THE LONG HAUL ❧

At the start of the 2012–13 season only three Premiership managers had been in charge of their respective clubs for ten years or more:

	Manager	Club	Appointed
1.	Sir Alex Ferguson	Man Utd	6 November 1986
2.	Arsene Wenger	Arsenal	30 September 1996
3.	David Moyes	Everton	15 March 2002

By the end of it, Ferguson had retired and been replaced by Moyes.

❧ THANKS FOR THE RELEGATION ❧

Following Watford's relegation from the FA Premier League in May 2007, the club handed Ady Boothroyd a new three-year contract.

❧ PREMIERSHIP TALK (15) ❧

"I have shaved my head. My flowing locks are now quite a bit shorter."
David Ginola *(Aston Villa)*

❧ FUTURE STARS ❧

When Avram Grant guided Maccabi Haifa to their first Liga Leumit (Israeli Championship) success in seven years in the 2000–01 season, his young side contained future Premiership stars Yossi Benayoun and Aiyegbeni Yakubu.

❧ THE MAGNIFICENT SEVEN RED DEVILS ❧

In 1995–96 Manchester United became the first English side to repeat the domestic Double, and achieved the feat with seven players from their previous Double triumph in 1993–94.

❧ EAGLES SWOOP BACK ❧

Crystal Palace became the first team to be relegated from and promoted back to the Premier League when they won the Division One title in 1994. The Eagles were relegated at the end of the inaugural Premiership campaign in 1992–93 along with Middlesbrough and Nottingham Forest. However, Forest also joined the Eagles in the Premiership for the 1994–95 season after finishing second in Division One, while Middlesbrough could only manage ninth in Division One. Amazingly it was Crystal Palace's and Nottingham Forest's first season under the management of Alan Smith and Frank Clark respectively, while Bryan Robson left Manchester United to take charge of Middlesbrough when the 1993–94 season ended.

❧ LIFE AFTER CLOUGHIE ❧

After achieving promotion back to the Premiership at the first attempt, Nottingham Forest finished third in the Premiership table in 1994–95 to win a UEFA Cup slot, their first European campaign of the post-Heysel era. Frank Clarke's side was helped by the goalscoring exploits of their striker Stan Collymore, who netted 22 Premiership goals. However, Collymore left the City Ground at the end of the season and moved to Anfield for £8.5 million.

⚜ O'LEARY SACKED ⚜

When Leeds United travelled met Cardiff City at Ninian Park in the FA Cup third round in January 2002, they were top of the Premier League table. However, the Welsh club, mid-table in Division Two, caused a huge upset, winning 2–1. Although Leeds finished fifth at the end of the season manager David O'Leary was sacked after four years in charge at Elland Road. Many people close to the club blamed O'Leary's book *Leeds United: On Trial* for the Irishman's departure, claiming that it destroyed morale in the dressing-room.

⚜ NEW HOMES ⚜

Eight out of the 20 Premier League clubs in 2012–13 played in stadiums that were less than 20 years old. This is the list:

Stadium	Club	Opened
Liberty Stadium	Swansea City	2007
Emirates Stadium	Arsenal	2006
Etihad Stadium (Eastlands))	Manchester City	2002
St Mary's Stadium	Southampton	2001
DW Stadium (JJB Stadium)	Wigan Athletic	1999
Madejski Stadium	Reading	1998
Britannia Stadium	Stoke City	1997
Stadium of Light	Sunderland	1997

⚜ PAISLEY'S LAST BATTLE ⚜

On 14 February 1996, the legendary Liverpool manager Bob Paisley died aged 77 after a four-year battle against cancer. Paisley won an astonishing 21 trophies between 1974 and 1983 and at the time of his death he was the most successful manager in English football. Sir Alex Ferguson has since taken over his mantle.

⚜ GUNNERS GIVEN A LESSON IN STYLE ⚜

On 25 February 2001, Manchester United annihilated their nearest challengers for the Premiership crown, Arsenal, 6–1 at Old Trafford.

⚜ ROBBIE RICH ⚜

On 1 November 1994, Liverpool handed Robbie Fowler, then aged 19, a contract that made him football's first teenage millionaire.

❧ 2007–08 BARCLAYS GOLDEN GLOVE AWARD ❧

This award was presented for the third successive season to Liverpool's Jose Reina, who kept 18 clean sheets in 38 Premiership games. David James – the all-time clean-sheet leader in Premier League history – came second with 17 clean sheets from 35 matches.

❧ SPURS HANDED RECORD FINE ❧

During the 1993–94 season, Tottenham Hotspur were the subject of a Football Association investigation that focused on financial irregularities that had occurred at the club during the 1980s when Irving Scholar had been the club's chairman. The club was found guilty and the FA handed out the heaviest financial penalty ever received by an English club, a fine of £600,000, deducted 12 Premiership points for the 1994–95 season and banned them from the 1994–95 FA Cup. Alan Sugar, the chairman of the club, appealed against the FA's ruling and succeeded in having it quashed – apart from the fine, which was increased to £1.5 million.

❧ QPR TOP DOGS IN THE CAPITAL ❧

Queen's Park Rangers, managed by former QPR and England captain Gerry Francis, ended the 1992–93 Premier League season in fifth place, highest of all the London clubs. Disappointingly for them, although fifth place was previously good enough for a UEFA Cup place, UEFA had not yet given back all of England's European competition places taken away following the 1985 Heysel disaster.

❧ RECORD-BUSTING RIO ❧

After failing to win the Premiership title for the first time in four seasons in 2001–02, Manchester United broke the British record transfer fee in July 2002 by shelling out £29.1 million for Leeds United centre-half Rio Ferdinand. It made him the most expensive defender in the world, as well as Britain's most expensive player for the second time in two seasons.

❧ SPREADING THE SCORING ❧

Although 2000–01 Premier League champions Manchester United were also the league's top scorers with 79 goals, no United players were in the top five of the goalscoring charts at the season's end.

❧ OLD BOYS NETWORK ❧

The following table lists the 2012–13 Premier League clubs in order of seniority:

Team	Founded	Age
Stoke City	1863	149
Reading	1871	141
Aston Villa	1874	138
Everton	1878	134
Manchester United	1878	134
West Bromwich Albion	1878	134
Sunderland	1879	133
Fulham	1879	133
Manchester City	1880	132
Tottenham Hotspur	1882	130
Southampton	1885	127
Arsenal	1886	126
Queens Park Rangers	1886	126
Liverpool	1892	120
Newcastle United	1892	120
West Ham United	1895	117
Norwich City	1902	110
Chelsea	1905	107
Swansea City	1912	100
Wigan Athletic	1932	80

❧ FORZA ZOLA ❧

Chelsea's Gianfranco Zola was voted Player of the Year by both the Professional Footballers' Association and the Football Writers' Association in 1996–97, when he also helped the Blues to FA Cup success.

❧ SAINTLY BRILLIANCE ❧

In 1994–95 the unfancied Southampton surprised many football pundits by avoiding relegation to finish tenth in the Premier League, mostly thanks to the sheer brilliance of Matt Le Tissier. The Saints ended the campaign higher than more-fancied teams such as Chelsea (11th), Arsenal (12th) and Everton (15th). However, at the end of the season the Southampton manager Alan Ball packed his bags and took over at Manchester City, leaving long-serving coach Dave Merrington in charge at The Dell.

♊ FINAL PREMIERSHIP TABLE 2002–2003 ♊

Pos Team	P	W	D	L	F	A	Pts
1. Manchester United (C)	38	25	8	5	74	34	83
2. Arsenal	38	23	9	6	85	42	78
3. Newcastle United	38	21	6	11	63	48	69
4. Chelsea	38	19	10	9	68	38	67
5. Liverpool	38	18	10	10	61	41	64
6. Blackburn Rovers	38	16	12	10	52	43	60
7. Everton	38	17	8	13	48	49	59
8. Southampton	38	13	13	12	43	46	52
9. Manchester City	38	15	6	17	47	54	51
10. Tottenham	38	14	8	16	51	62	50
11. Middlesbrough	38	13	10	15	48	44	49
12. Charlton Athletic	38	14	7	17	45	56	49
13. Birmingham City	38	13	9	16	41	49	48
14. Fulham	38	13	9	16	41	50	48
15. Leeds United	38	14	5	19	58	57	47
16. Aston Villa	38	12	9	17	42	47	45
17. Bolton Wanderers	38	10	14	14	41	51	44
18. West Ham United (R)	38	10	12	16	42	59	42
19. West Bromwich Albion (R)	38	6	8	24	29	65	26
20. Sunderland (R)	38	4	7	27	21	65	19

♊ THAT'S ENTERTAINMENT ♊

A highlight of the 2007–08 season was an exhilarating encounter at Fratton Park in which Portsmouth beat Reading 7–4, with Benjani Mwaruwari scoring a hat-trick for Portsmouth. Although the 11-goal aggregate was a Premiership record for a single match, the total could have been higher still. During the game Marcus Hahnemann, Reading's American goalkeeper, saved a point-blank shot from Glen Johnson; David James in the Pompey goal saved a penalty from Nicky Shorey; and a goal was disallowed for offside. Benjani only played because Kanu was injured.

♊ RACE TO STAY UP ♊

Bolton Wanderers, Manchester City and Queen's Park Rangers were relegated from the Premier League in 1995–96. City needed to beat Liverpool in their final game, but somehow the wrong message went out to the players, who appeared to be playing for a draw late in the match, thinking a single point would be good enough for survival.

☙ JEEPERS KEEPERS ☙

On 14 October 2006, Chelsea goalkeepers Petr Cech and Carlo Cudicini both sustained head injuries during their match against Reading. Cech underwent surgery for a depressed skull fracture, while the more fortunate Cudicini was treated and released from hospital the same evening.

☙ UNITED KEANE TO BREAK THE BANK ☙

Before the start of the 1993–94 season, Roy Keane became the most expensive player in British football history. The Nottingham Forest and Republic of Ireland hard man left relegated Nottingham Forest and joined the reigning Premier League champions, Manchester United, for a fee of £3.75 million. The 22-year-old had turned down offers from Arsenal and Blackburn Rovers to join Alex Ferguson's exciting side.

☙ INTERNATIONAL EAGLES ☙

In season 1997–98 Crystal Palace added internationals Michele Padovano (Italy) and Tomas Brolin (Sweden) to their team, which already had the Italian Attilio Lombardo in the heart of their midfield. However, the international trio could not save Palace from a quick return to Division One. Lombardo had enjoyed considerable success in Italian football, winning the the European Cup Winners' Cup (1990), Coppa Italia (1991 and 1994), Serie A (1991) and the Supercoppa Italia (1991) during his time with Sampdoria (1989–95). With Juventus (1995–97) he won the UEFA Champions League (1996), the World Club Championship (1996) and the European Super Cup (1996).

☙ OLD BOYS REUNION ☙

In December 1998, Brian Kidd left his assistant manager's job under Alex Ferguson at Manchester United and took charge of Blackburn Rovers, who had sacked manager Roy Hodgson in November. Kidd brought former Manchester United hero Brian McClair to Ewood Park from Motherwell as his assistant. In his first month at Blackburn, Kidd won the Premier League Manager of the Month Award, but Rovers were relegated to Division One after drawing 0–0 with Manchester United at Ewood Park in their penultimate game of the season.

※ PREMIERSHIP TALK (16) ※

"My best moment? I have a lot of good moments, but the one I prefer is when I kicked the hooligan."
Eric Cantona (Manchester United)

※ GIGGSY HITS CENTURY ※

When Ryan Giggs scored Manchester United's opening goal in their 4–1 win over Derby County in the Premier League at Old Trafford on 8 December 2007, it was his 100th league goal for the Red Devils. Derby's goal was their first in nine Premiership away games, in which they had conceded 24 goals.

※ "JUDAS" SIGNS FOR THE REDS ※

Prior to the start of the 2000–01 season, Nick Barmby became the first Everton player in more than 40 years to move across Stanley Park, when he joined the Reds in a £6m transfer deal. At the time Barmby claimed he loved Liverpool more than Everton, which angered Blues fans. In the Merseyside derby on 29 October 2000 Barmby ran out at Anfield to cries of "Judas!" from the Everton fans. Barmby silenced the Blues by scoring in a 3–1 win for Liverpool. In August 2002, Barmby was sold for £2.75 million to Leeds United.

※ WISE MOVE ※

David May left Blackburn Rovers prior to the start of the 1994–95 season and joined Manchester United. His move may not have looked like a good decision at the end of the season when Rovers pipped United to the Premiership title, but May went on to have a successful career with United, one that saw him win many trophies including the famous Treble in 1999.

※ HOULLIER WALKS ALONE ※

Liverpool brought in the former French national coach Gerard Houllier at the start of the 1998–99 season to act as joint manager of the club alongside Roy Evans. However, Evans was unhappy with the arrangement and quit in November 1998. The Anfield club could only manage seventh place in the Premiership in 1998–99, which was the club's worst league finish in five years and not good enough to secure European football.

❧ ANCIENT MONUMENTS ☙

Ten of the 20 Premier League clubs in 2012–13 – one half of them
– had played at the same home ground for more than 100 years.
They were:

Club	Stadium	Year Built
Liverpool	Anfield	1884
Everton	Goodison Park	1892
Newcastle United	St James' Park	1892
Fulham	Craven Cottage	1896
Aston Villa	Villa Park	1897
Tottenham Hotspur	White Hart Lane	1899
West Bromwich Albion	The Hawthorns	1900
Queens Park Rangers	Loftus Road	1904
West Ham United	Upton Park	1904
Chelsea	Stamford Bridge	1905

❧ POMPEY'S GREAT ESCAPE ☙

With ten games remaining in the 2005–06 Premiership season,
it seemed certain that Portsmouth would be relegated. They were
eight points from safety, but following the return of manager
Harry Redknapp they strung together a series of good results
to steer them to safety at the expense of West Bromwich Albion
and Birmingham City with a game to go (Sunderland's fate was
already sealed).

❧ SPEAKING OUT ☙

In August 2006, Leeds United chairman Ken Bates, formerly the
chairman of Chelsea, reported the London club to the Football
Association, the FA Premier League and FIFA over the alleged
tapping-up of three Leeds youth-team players.

❧ CHELSEA'S TREBLE ☙

In 1995–96 Chelsea finished 11th for the third time in four seasons.

❧ PREMIERSHIP TALK (17) ☙

"We have top players and, sorry if I'm arrogant, we have a top manager."
Former Chelsea manager Jose Mourinho

✄ WALK-OUT FOR THE SPECIAL ONE ✄

At half-time during Chelsea's 0–0 draw with Fulham in the Premiership on 29 September 2007, a number of Chelsea fans walked out of Stamford Bridge in protest over Jose Mourinho's departure from the club.

✄ THE LITTLE FELLA ✄

In October 1995, Bryan Robson paid Sao Paulo £4.75 million for the services of their diminutive 22-year-old Brazilian striker Juninho Paulista. Juninho was an instant success at the Riverside Stadium and went on to inscribe his name in the club's history books as one of their greatest-ever players. Juninho stood just 1.67 metres tall and during his time on Teeside became known to Boro fans as "TLF (The Little Fella)".

✄ BACK IN WORK ✄

In September 1996, Howard Wilkinson was sacked as the manager of Leeds United after suffering a 4–0 home defeat at the hands of Manchester United. George Graham, himself sacked as the manager of Arsenal on 21 February 1995, took over the reins at Elland Road. Graham had been banned by the FA for a year after he admitted having accepted a "bung" from the Norwegian football agent Rune Hauge.

✄ WENGER MISCALCULATES SHIFT IN POWER ✄

When Arsenal, the defending Premiership champions, enjoyed a good start to the 2002–03 Premier League season, their manager Arsene Wenger talked about a shift in power from Manchester to North London. However, Sir Alex Ferguson's side made the Frenchman rue his words by reclaiming the Premiership crown at the end of the season with Arsenal finishing runners-up to United for the fourth time in five seasons.

✄ GOD ARRIVES AT ANFIELD ✄

Robbie Fowler, aged 18, scored in his first-team debut for Liverpool, a 3–1 League Cup first-round, first-leg win over Fulham at Craven Cottage on 22 September 1993. He went on to score 12 Premiership goals in 28 games that season. Reds fans later nicknamed him "God".

⚡ AFRICAN PREMIER LEAGUE FANTASY XI ⚡

1
Bruce
GROBBELAAR
(ZIMBABWE)

2
Emmanuel
EBOUE
(IVORY COAST)

6
Lucas
RADEBE
(SOUTH AFRICA, capt.)

5
Christopher
SAMBA
(REP. OF CONGO)

3
Kolo
TOURE
(IVORY COAST)

7
GEREMI
(CAMEROON)

4
Michael
ESSIEN
(GHANA)

8
Yaya
TOURE
(IVORY COAST)

9
George
WEAH
(LIBERIA)

10
Didier
DROGBA
(IVORY COAST)

11
JJ
OKOCHA
(NIGERIA)

Substitutes

Richard *KINGSON (Ghana)* • Radhi *JAIDE (Tunisia)* • Freddie *KANOUTE (Mali)* •
Benni *McCARTHY (S. Africa)* • Adel *TAARABT (Morocco)* • *YAKUBU (Nigeria)* •
El Hadji *DIOUF (Senegal)*

Manager

John *FASHANU (English but of Yoruba Nigerian descent on his father's side)*

Did You Know That?
In November 1994 John Fashanu and Bruce Grobbelaar were accused of match fixing along with Hans Segers and a Malaysian businessman named Heng Suan Lim.

⚡ PREMIER MEDAL COLLECTOR ⚡

Manchester United's Ryan Giggs has won more Premier League winners' medals, 13, than any other player (1993, 1994, 1996, 1997, 1999, 2000, 2001, 2003, 2007, 2008, 2009, 2011 and 2013). United's ninth title in 2006–07 also placed Giggs as the all-time leading medal winner in English top flight, passing the eight First Division winners' medals collected by Alan Hansen with Liverpool.

⚡ LITTLE BIG MAN ⚡

In 1995–96 Brian Little guided Aston Villa to League Cup glory and fourth place in the Premiership.

⚘ OVAL BALLS WELCOME HERE ⚘

Ground-sharing is not a new phenomenon. Wimbledon left Plough Lane long before the Premiership began, spending eight Premiership seasons at Crystal Palace's Selhurst Park. Manchester United's Old Trafford has hosted Rugby League's Super League Grand Final every year since 1998. These Premier League clubs have shared their homes for at least half a season with other sports since 1992:

Club	Stadium	Occupier	Sport
Bradford City	Valley Parade	Bradford Bulls	Rugby League
Charlton Athletic	The Valley	London Broncos	Rugby League
Chelsea	Stamford Bridge	London Monarchs	US Football
Hull City	KC Stadium	Hull FC	Rugby League
Queens Park Rangers	Loftus Road	London Wasps	Rugby Union
Reading	Majdeski Stadium	London Irish	Rugby Union
Swansea City	Liberty Stadium	Ospreys	Rugby Union
Tottenham Hotspur	White Hart Lane	London Monarchs	US Football
Watford	Vicarage Road	Saracens	Rugby Union
Wigan Athletic	DW Stadium	Wigan Warriors	Rugby League

Did You Know That?
Manchester City moved into the venue which hosted the 2002 Commonwealth Games athletics events (then the City of Manchester Stadium, now the Eithad) and West Ham United have been given the green light to redevelop and move into the Olympic Stadium where the London 2012 Olympic Games athletics were held.

⚘ A RUUD DEPARTURE ⚘

On 12 February 1998, Chelsea sacked their manager Ruud Gullit following a bust-up between the Dutch superstar and the club's chairman Ken Bates. Gianluca Vialli, their 33-year-old Italian striker, took charge of first-team affairs as player-manager. Over the next three months Vialli guided the Blues to victory in both the Coca-Cola Cup and the European Cup Winners' Cup. The Italian theme continued in the Premiership during the 1997–98 season: when Steve Coppell vacated his position as manager of Crystal Palace, moving upstairs to be director of football at Selhurst Park, he was replaced by the Eagles' 31-year-old midfielder Attillo Lombardo as player-manager (along with Tomas Brolin). However, the Brolin/Lombardo tenure only lasted until the end of the season, when Terry Venables took charge.

⚜ THE TIGHTEST FINISH ⚜

The 2011–12 season ended with Manchester City deposing neighbours United as Premier League champions, ending a 44-year wait for the title. The Reds had seemingly secured their 20th top-flight championship when they led City by eight points with six games each to play. City won their next five matches, including 1–0 against United at the Etihad to join the Reds on 86 points but with a better goal difference of eight, +63 to +55. On the final day of the season, City needed to do better against relegation-threatened Queens Park Rangers than United did against Sunderland. United beat the Black Cats 1–0 and celebrated the championship as news of City losing 2–1 came through. But City scored twice in the dying moments to win 3–2 and snatch the title, the first Premiership decided by goal difference.

⚜ THE TINKERMAN IS TINKERED WITH ⚜

After guiding Chelsea to the semi-finals of the UEFA Champions League and runners-up position in the Premier League in season 2003–04, the Blues' highest league finish since their 1955 title, Claudio Ranieri was rewarded with the sack. The man nicknamed the "Tinkerman" by the English media was replaced by Jose Mourinho.

⚜ NO WAY TO TREAT A KNIGHT ⚜

At the end of August 2004, just four games into the season, Newcastle United sacked manager Sir Bobby Robson and replaced him with the Blackburn Rovers manager Graeme Souness.

⚜ QUEEN'S APPOINTMENT ⚜

On 24 November 1993, the Queens Park Rangers manager, Gerry Francis, was tipped to take over from Graham Taylor as England manager after Taylor quit his post as the national team boss following England's failure to qualify for the 1994 World Cup finals. However, Francis was overlooked in favour of a former QPR manager, Terry Venables.

⚜ SIR ALEX THE GREAT ⚜

In the 2002–03 season Sir Alex Ferguson won the Barclaycard Manager of the Year Award after guiding Manchester United to their eighth Premiership title.

⚜ PREMIERSHIP TALK (18) ⚜

"Sometimes in football you have to score goals."
Thierry Henry *(Arsenal)*

⚜ HAPPY 125TH BIRTHDAY ⚜

Prior to their home game against Aston Villa at White Hart Lane on 1 October 2007, Tottenham Hotspur celebrated their 125th anniversary with a parade of legends before kick-off. However, the Villains looked set to burst Spurs' party bubble when they took a 4–1 lead after going a goal down. But Spurs fought back and scored three more goals to earn a point from the 4–4 thriller leaving them two places off the foot of the Premiership table after eight games of the season had been played.

⚜ NEW BHOY IN TOWN ⚜

Martin O'Neill resigned as manager of Leicester City after guiding them to eighth in the Premiership (their best finish since the league was formed) and League Cup glory at Wembley (for the second time during his reign) at the end of the 1999–2000 season. He moved north of the border to take charge at Glasgow Celtic. The Bhoys achieved much success under O'Neill's astute leadership. Peter Taylor left Gillingham to succeed O'Neill at Leicester.

⚜ CANARIES KNOCKED OFF THEIR PERCH ⚜

On 26 January 2013.Norwich City suffered the embarrassment of being the first Premier League club to lose to non-League opposition in the FA Cup. Luton Town, who were relegated from the top flight a year before the Premiership started, and now play the Conference Premier, won 1–0 at Carrow Road, thanks to a goal from Scott Rendell.

⚜ THE SPECIAL ONE LIVES UP TO HIS NAME ⚜

Jose Mourinho, nicknamed the "Special One", lived up to the tag in his first season in charge of Chelsea, guiding the Blues to the Premier League title. It was Chelsea's first Championship success since they won the First Division in 1955. Chelsea were in superb form all season, and hardly any team could live with them as they racked up a Premiership record of 95 points (29 wins, 8 draws and 1 defeat) and a unique defensive record of only 15 league goals conceded.

☙ AUSTRALIA PREMIER LEAGUE FANTASY XI ☙

1
Mark
SCHWARZER
(FULHAM)

2
Lucas
NEILL
(WEST HAM, capt)

5
Brett
EMERTON
(BLACKBURN)

6
Craig
MOORE
(NEWCASTLE UTD)

3
Jacob
BURNS
(BLACKPOOL)

7
Luke
WILKSHIRE
(MIDDLESBROUGH)

4
Danny
TIATTO
(MAN CITY)

8
Stan
LAZARIDIS
(BIRMINGHAM)

9
Tim
CAHILL
(EVERTON)

10
Mark
VIDUKA
(NEWCASTLE UTD)

11
Harry
KEWELL
(LIVERPOOL)

Substitutes

Adam *FEDERICI* (READING) • Josip *SKOKO* (WIGAN) • Hayden *FOXE* (WEST HAM) •
Brett *HOLMAN* (ASTON VILLA) • Robbie *SLATER* (SOUTHAMPTON) •
Paul *OKON* (MIDDLESBROUGH) • Tony *VIDMAR* (MIDDLESBROUGH)

Manager

Terry *VENABLES*

Did You Know That?

Terry Venables became manager of Australia in November 1996, and almost took the side to the 1998 World Cup finals – Australia lost their final play-off match against Iran on away goals.

☙ GUNNERS ON THE MOVE ☙

At the end of their 2001–02 Double-winning season Arsenal chairman Peter Hill-Wood revealed the club would move into its new 60,000-capacity stadium at the start of the 2004–05 season.

☙ BACK IN THE FIZZ ☙

At the end of the 2006–07 Premier League season, two of the three promoted clubs, Sheffield United and Watford, dropped back into the Coca-Cola Championship along with Charlton Athletic, whose eight-year Premiership tenure came to an end.

❧ FINAL PREMIERSHIP TABLE 2003–2004 ❧

Pos	Team	P	W	D	L	F	A	Pts
1.	Arsenal (C)	38	26	12	0	73	26	90
2.	Chelsea	38	24	7	7	67	30	79
3.	Manchester United	38	23	6	9	64	35	75
4.	Liverpool	38	16	12	10	55	37	60
5.	Newcastle United	38	13	17	8	52	40	56
6.	Aston Villa	38	15	11	12	48	44	56
7.	Charlton Athletic	38	14	11	13	51	51	53
8.	Bolton Wanderers	38	14	11	13	48	56	53
9.	Fulham	38	14	10	14	52	46	52
10.	Birmingham City	38	12	14	12	43	48	50
11.	Middlesbrough	38	13	9	16	44	52	48
12.	Southampton	38	12	11	15	44	45	47
13.	Portsmouth	38	12	9	17	47	54	45
14.	Tottenham Hotspur	38	13	6	19	47	57	45
15.	Blackburn Rovers	38	12	8	18	51	59	44
16.	Manchester City	38	9	14	15	55	54	41
17.	Everton	38	9	12	17	45	57	39
18.	Leicester City (R)	38	6	15	17	48	65	33
19.	Leeds United (R)	38	8	9	21	40	79	33
20.	Wolverhampton Wanderers (R)	38	7	12	19	38	77	33

❧ NO CHRISTMAS CHEER FOR LAWRIE ❧

On 21 December 2007, Fulham sacked their manager, Lawrie Sanchez, who had only taken over the club from Chris Coleman in April 2007 (originally on a caretaker basis). He became the seventh Premier League manager to leave or be removed from his post in the 2007–08 season. The club were struggling in 18th place in the Premiership, having won just two games all season.

❧ CRAZY GANGS HIT LOW ❧

Wimbledon finished 14th in the Premiership in 1995–96, their lowest placing since joining the big guns a decade earlier.

❧ LAST GOAL STANDING ❧

Julian Dicks was the last Liverpool player to score in front of the standing Kop. On 9 April 1994 Dicks converted a penalty in Liverpool's 1–0 Premiership win over Ipswich Town. (117)

♚ SOLE CASUALTY ♛

Bolton Wanderers' Roy McFarland was the only Premiership manager to lose his job during the 1995–96 season, although Southampton's Dave Merrington, who had helped the Saints avoid the drop, was also relieved of his duties in June 1996.

♚ WOEFUL CITY ♛

Of the clubs newly promoted to the Premiership at the start of the 2000–01 season Manchester City was the only one to suffer relegation back to Division One at the end of it. It was the Blues' fourth relegation in a seven-year period that had also seen them fall into Division Two for a season. Shortly afterwards, they sacked their manager Joe Royle.

♚ EVERY GAME PLAYED AWAY ♛

During the 2002–03 season Fulham played their home games at Queen's Park Rangers' Loftus Road ground as Craven Cottage was being upgraded. Loftus Road witnessed the lowest Premier League attendance of the season when a crowd of 14,017 paid to see Fulham play Blackburn Rovers.

♚ SKY BLUES HIT ORBIT ♛

Going into the 1994–95 season Coventry City made Manchester United's Dion Dublin their record transfer purchase at £2 million to take him from Old Trafford to Highfield Road.

♚ QUICK OFF THE MARK ♛

Robbie Fowler scored the fastest ever Premier League hat-trick when he bagged three against Arsenal at Anfield on 28 August 1994 in only four minutes and 33 seconds, just before the half-hour mark. Liverpool won the game 3–0.

♚ SEVENTH HEAVEN FOR BLACK CATS ♛

Sunderland finished seventh in the Premiership table in the 2000–01 season for the second year in a row. The Black Cats looked on course for at least a UEFA Cup place when they were lying second behind Manchester United in early February, but they fell away at the end.

♘ MICHAEL OWEN ♞

Michael James Owen was born on 14 December 1979 in Hawarden, Cheshire. His father Terry played for Everton, so it was no surprise that Michael grew up supporting Everton, nor that his boyhood hero was Everton and England striker Gary Lineker. When he was seven years old, his dad persuaded the manager of Mold Alexandra to allow Michael to play for their team, an Under-11 side. Michael signed schoolboy forms with Liverpool aged 13 and attended Lilleshall's School of Excellence. As a 16-year-old he was in Liverpool's FA Youth Cup-winning team and, just after his 17th birthday, Michael signed professional terms with the Reds.

In May 1997, Michael made his Liverpool debut against Wimbledon, scoring in a 2–1 defeat. He was a regular starter in 1997–98, ending the season as the club's joint top scorer with 18 goals, and being voted the PFA Young Player of the Year. He also made a sensational arrival on the international scene at the 1998 World Cup finals. After 23 goals in 40 games for Liverpool in 1998–99, a niggling hamstring injury made the following season one to forget. But, in 2000–01, he helped Liverpool to League Cup, UEFA Cup and FA Cup success, scoring both of Liverpool's goals in their 2–1 FA Cup win over Arsenal.

Michael won FA Charity Shield and European Super Cup winners' medals in 2001–02 and became the first English player since Kevin Keegan to win the Ballon d'Or, the European Footballer of the Year Award. On 21 December 2001, he scored his 100th goal for Liverpool, and bagged his 100th Premier League goal the following season.

In August 2004, Michael joined Real Madrid for £8 million, but the move was not a huge success, though he scored 16 times in 41 outings, many as a substitute. He returned to England a year later, becoming Newcastle United's record signing, the club paying £16 million for him. He scored his first goal for the Magpies in his second game for the club, but his appearances were limited by a succession of injuries, most notably the one to his cruciate ligament during the 2012 World Cup..

Michael joined Manchester United in 2009 and finally won a Championship winners' medal when he helped United clinch the 2010–11 Premiership (he also won the League Cup with United in 2010). In September 2012, Michael moved to Stoke City and retired in 2013.

On the interntional stage he scored 40 goals in 88 England games.

Did You Know That?
One week after scoring for Liverpool against Oliver Kahn of Bayern Munich in the 2001 European Super Cup, Michael bagged a hat-trick against him in England's 5–1 win over Germany in Munich.

❧ JAMES BOND ROLE AT NEWCASTLE ❧

On 1 October 2007, Newcastle United strenuously denied claims made in a Sunday national tabloid newspaper of a bugging scandal within the club. The newspaper published claims by Brian Tough, a former security consultant for the club who was initially hired as a bodyguard for Douglas Hall, the son of the Magpies' one-time owner Sir John Hall. Tough claimed that he was paid £40,000 a year to bug the phones of former manager Kevin Keegan, former Sunderland chairman Bob Murray and others. Freddy Shepherd, who was chairman at St James' Park at the time when the bugging was alleged to have taken place, denied any involvement in the allegations, saying: "This is James Bond stuff. I certainly didn't employ anyone in 007 activities at St James' Park. Mr Tough was never employed by me or the club." A club spokesman added: "If the club has been the victim of any criminal activity, the club will take appropriate action."

❧ GROUND SHARE OPPOSTION ❧

During the 2001–02 season, Everton announced plans to move away from their Goodison Park home and relocate to a brand new all-seater stadium with a 55,000 capacity on the banks of the River Mersey. There was talk of a ground share with Liverpool, leading to fans of both clubs jamming radio phone-ins with their vociferous objections to any such partnership. One Everton fan went on the air and said he wouldn't share a Twix with a Liverpool fan, never mind a football stadium.

❧ LAST-GASP SIGNING ❧

On 31 August 2002, the date of the transfer deadline, Robbie Keane left Leeds United and joined Tottenham Hotspur.

❧ ARCH RIVAL TAKES CHARGE AT THE LANE ❧

In September 1998 Tottenham Hotspur sacked manager Christian Gross, who had been in charge at White Hart Lane for less than a year. A month later Spurs appointed the former Arsenal and Leeds manager George Graham as his replacement. The golden touch that Graham enjoyed at Arsenal as manager returned in his first season in charge of Spurs as he guided the team to League Cup success and only their second European campaign since 1985.

❧ GOOD GUYS AND BAD GUYS ❧

Blackpool had the best disciplinary record in the 2010–11 Premier League with just 53 points (47 yellow and two red cards). In contrast, Manchester City had the worst overall disciplinary record, with 89 points (74 yellow and five red cards). That said, Newcastle United (75 yellows) and West Bromwich Albion (seven reds) did worse than City in those categories.

❧ ALL CHANGE AGAIN AT ANFIELD ❧

In October 2010, after three years in charge, but amid increasing turmoil and rumours of financial meltdown, joint owners Tom Hicks and George Gillett sold their stake in Liverpool to John Henry of the New England Sports Ventures (Fenway Sports Group). Henry, like his predecessors, owned sports franchises in the USA – his being the famous baseball club the Boston Red Sox.

❧ VAN DER SAR'S WORLD RECORD ❧

Edwin van der Sar was almost unbeatable for more than one-third of the 2008–09 season. The Netherlands' most capped player – he finished with 130 appearances for the Dutch national team – went 1,311 minutes without conceding a Premier League goal (with clean sheets in the FA Cup and UEFA Champion League, the overall total was 1,491). It started after Samir Nasri's second goal 48 minutes into Arsenal's 2–1 victory at the Emirates on 8 November 2008 and ended almost four months later, on 4 March 2009, when Peter Lovenkrands netted an eighth-minute goal for Newcastle United at St James' Park. He kept a world record 14 consecutive single-season League clean sheets, beating Jose Maria Buljubasich's mark set in the Chilean league in 2005. As well as receiving a Barclays Merit award for this achievement, van der Sar also won the Golden Gloves award.after the season.

❧ THE SAD TALE OF THE THREE ROBERTOS ❧

In August 2012, three Premiership managers were named Roberto: Di Matteo had just won the UEFA Champions League with Chelsea, Mancini had guided Manchester City to the 2011–12 title and Wigan's Martinez had won a relegation battle. By the end of the following season, both Di Matteo and Mancini had been sacked and Martinez, despite winning the FA Cup, suffered relegation before resigning to become the new Everton boss.

❧ CITY FEELING THE BLUES ❧

At the end of the 1997–98 season, Manchester City (who had been in the Premier League between 1992 and 1997) were relegated for the second time in successive seasons, dropping from Premiership football to Division Two. City went into their final game of the season, against Stoke City at Stoke's new Britannia Stadium, knowing that a win for either team might see them avoid relegation. In fact Man City beat Stoke City 5–2, but both clubs were relegated (along with bottom-placed Reading) because the three teams above the drop zone all won their games. It was the first time in the club's history that the Citizens suffered relegation to the third tier of the English Football League, and their fans, together with the Stoke City fans, marked their last day in Division One with disgraceful violence after the game.

❧ A NEW HOME ❧

Middlesbrough, First Division champions in 1994–95, went into the 1995–96 season with a new home. The club left Ayresome Park and moved to the purpose-built Riverside Stadium, the first new stadium in English football's top flight in 72 years.

❧ LEEDS SMASH CLUB'S PIGGY BANK ❧

In November 2000, Leeds United broke the English transfer record when they handed over £18 million to West Ham United for their 22-year-old centre-half Rio Ferdinand. The previous record was set by Newcastle United in January 1995 when they forked out £15 million to Blackburn Rovers for Alan Shearer, and the Geordies' spending was equalled by Chelsea in May 2000 when they brought Jimmy Floyd Hasselbaink to Stamford Bridge from Atletico Madrid.

❧ UNLUCKY TOFFEES ❧

On the final day of the 2001–02 season, David Moyes' first full season in charge at Goodison Park, Everton were in contention for a top-six finish and with it a UEFA Cup place in season 2003–04. However, they lost their last game of the season to the champions, Manchester United, 2–1 at Goodison Park. The defeat saw Everton finish seventh in the table, and European qualification went to Blackburn Rovers, who finished one point above them.

❧ NORDIC PREMIER LEAGUE FANTASY XI ❧

1
Peter
SCHMEICHEL
(DENMARK)

2
Daniel
AGGER
(DENMARK)

6
Olof
MELBERG
(SWEDEN, capt.)

5
Ronny
JOHNSEN
(NORWAY)

3
John Arne
RIISE
(NORWAY)

7
Jari
LITMANEN
(FINLAND)

4
Jan
MOLBY
(DENMARK)

8
Eidur
GUDJOHNSEN
(ICELAND)

10
Ole Gunnar
SOLSKJAER
(NORWAY)

9
Brian
LAUDRUP
(DENMARK)

11
Jesper
BLOMQVIST
(SWEDEN)

Substitutes

Thomas *SORENSEN (Denmark)* • Stig Inge *BJØRNEBYE (Norway)* •
Sami *HYPPIA (Finland)* • Mikael *FORRSSEL (Finland)* • Tore Andre *FLO (Norway)* •
Henrik *LARSSON (Sweden)* • Freddie *LJUNGBERG (Sweden)*

Manager

Michael *LAUDRUP (Denmark)*

Did You Know That?
Michael (104 caps) and younger brother Brian Laudrup (82) never played together at club level, though both were at Brondby and Ajax.

❧ BLUES' EUROPEAN HAT-TRICK ❧

Chelsea's player-manager Gianluca Vialli guided the Blues to third place in the Premiership and European Super Cup glory in. At the end of the season the 35-year-old Italian hung up his boots to concentrate on coaching. Third-place (and a place in the Champions League play-offs) secured a third-consecutive season of European football for the Stamford Bridge outfit.

❧ OSSIE GETS THE BOOT ❧

Tottenham Hotspur sacked Ossie Ardiles as manager in November 1995 after they lost 3–0 to Notts County in the League Cup. Spurs appointed QPR's former manager Gerry Francis as their new boss.

♕ PREMIERSHIP TALK (19) ♛

"Football must be your priority. You don't need to live in London or Manchester to be happy; you don't need to be surrounded by expensive shops or fancy cafes. What's your priority – your wife and her shopping or your football? Or money? If a player doesn't want to come to Sunderland because his wife wants to go shopping in London, it's a sad state of affairs."

Roy Keane, Sunderland manager, August 2007

♕ ALMOST A RUUD SIGNING ♛

In the summer of 2000 Manchester United, the reigning champions, announced that the coveted PSV Eindhoven and Dutch international striker Ruud van Nistelrooy was set to join the Old Trafford side. However, van Nistelrooy subsequently failed a medical as a result of a knee injury and his move was put on hold for a year. Meanwhile Sir Alex Ferguson did get the United chequebook out and paid AS Monaco £7.8 million, a club record transfer fee for a goalkeeper, for the French 1998 World Cup winner Fabian Barthez.

♕ LIVERPOOL SLUMP ♛

Entering 2003 Liverpool lay sixth in the Premiership table, streets behind the eventual champions Manchester United, while their manager Gerard Houllier was suffering the worst run a Liverpool manager had had for almost half a century. In the end the Anfield side finished fifth in the table and outside the UEFA Champions League places.

♕ FIVE TROPHIES NOT GOOD ENOUGH ♛

At the start of the 2000–01 season Chelsea sacked manager Gianluca Vialli, despite the fact that the former Italian international striker had won five trophies since his appointment as player-manager in February 1998. Indeed, the fifth trophy was the 2001 FA Charity Shield victory over Manchester United in the last ever club game at Wembley Stadium before it was torn down and rebuilt.

♕ FOUR FROM FIVE FOR FERGIE ♛

In 1996–97 Alex Ferguson guided Manchester United to their fourth Premiership title in five seasons.

❧ REMEMBERING STAN ❧

Aston Villa captain Stilyan "Stan" Petrov announced that he was taking a break from football in March 2012 after being diagnosed with acute leukaemia. The midfielder, who previously played for Celtic and won more than 100 caps for Bulgaria, was a much-loved character. Villa fans showed their support for him for rising in the 19th minute of each match (he wore the No.19 shirt) and applauding him. In May 2013, Petrov, still fighting the condition, retired.

❧ EUELL DO NICELY ❧

Charlton Athletic broke the club's record transfer fee at the end of the 2000–01 season when they paid First Division Wimbledon £4.75 million for their highly prized striker Jason Euell. Throughout his career Euell, who is deaf in his left ear, has been a role model for many children who share his problem. Indeed, he has been an ambassador for the National Deaf Awareness in Sport Alliance since 2000 and is very active for the charity, taking part in various fundraising events.

❧ BANTAMS PUNCH ABOVE THEIR WEIGHT ❧

On the final day of the 1999–2000 Premiership season Bradford City played Liverpool at Valley Parade. Liverpool needed a victory to secure UEFA Champions League football, while the Bantams needed to win to retain their Premiership status. Bradford City, playing in English football's top flight for the first time since 1922, beat Liverpool 1–0 thanks to a goal from their defender David Weatherall. In the end Bradford beat the drop by three points, while Liverpool lost the third UEFA Champions League slot to Leeds United by two points.

❧ SIR BOBBY'S TOON ❧

In the 2001–02 season, Sir Bobby Robson guided Newcastle United to fourth in the Premiership table, their highest placing since 1997, and secured UEFA Champions League football for only the second time in the club's history.

❧ PIPPED AT THE POST ❧

Arsenal claimed the last UEFA Cup slot on the final day of the 1995–96 season by two points from Everton.

♕ WALTER'S REIGN ♕

In his first season in charge of Everton, Walter Smith guided the Merseyside club to 14th in the Premiership table. Prior to Smith's arrival at Goodison Park, he guided Glasgow Rangers to seven Scottish championships, three Scottish FA Cups and four Scottish League Cups.

♕ ISLAND SPICE ♕

There was always a little bit of added tension when Matt Le Tissier's Southampton played against a team with Graeme Le Saux in it. They were born just three days apart in October 1968 and both came from the Channel Islands, but "Le God" – as Saints fans dubbed him – is a Guernsey man, while Le Saux hails from neighbouring Jersey.

♕ PREMIERSHIP TALK (20) ♕

"Buying players for Chelsea is the hardest job in the Premier League."
Former Chelsea manager Jose Mourinho

♕ BLUES AND REDS CLEAN UP ♕

With Manchester United and Chelsea making a clean sweep of the 2006–07 season's domestic silverware (United won the Premier League title, while Chelsea won the League Cup and the FA Cup) it meant that Spurs (fifth), Everton (sixth) and Bolton Wanderers (seventh) all claimed UEFA Cup places for the 2007–08 season. Blackburn Rovers (tenth) qualified for the Intertoto Cup as the highest-placed team who applied for the competition but who failed to earn an automatic UEFA Cup spot, as both Reading (eighth) and Portsmouth (ninth) did not apply. Aston Villa nearly gained a place in the UEFA Cup via the European Fair Play League draw. Their name was placed in the hat by virtue of Spurs, the 2006–07 FA Premier League Fair Play winners, already having qualified for the competition, but Villa missed out, losing to the representatives from Finland and Norway.

♕ CHELSEA'S UNLUCKY DOZEN ♕

Chelsea endured a torrid sequence of 12 successive Premiership games without a win in the 1992–93 season, the worst run of winless games of any of the 22 teams that season.

✂ FINAL PREMIERSHIP TABLE 2004–2005 ✂

Pos Team	P	W	D	L	F	A	Pts
1. Chelsea (C)	38	29	8	1	72	15	95
2. Arsenal	38	25	8	5	87	36	83
3. Manchester United	38	22	11	5	57	26	77
4. Everton	38	18	7	13	45	46	61
5. Liverpool	38	17	7	14	52	41	58
6. Bolton Wanderers	38	16	10	12	49	44	58
7. Middlesbrough	38	14	13	11	53	46	55
8. Manchester City	38	13	13	12	47	39	52
9. Tottenham Hotspur	38	14	10	14	47	41	52
10. Aston Villa	38	12	11	15	45	52	47
11. Charlton Athletic	38	12	10	16	42	58	46
12. Birmingham City	38	11	12	15	40	46	45
13. Fulham	38	12	8	18	52	60	44
14. Newcastle United	38	10	14	14	47	57	44
15. Blackburn Rovers	38	9	15	14	32	43	42
16. Portsmouth	38	10	9	19	43	59	39
17. West Bromwich Albion	38	6	16	16	36	61	34
18. Crystal Palace (R)	38	7	12	19	41	62	33
19. Norwich City (R)	38	7	12	19	42	77	33
20. Southampton (R)	38	6	14	18	45	66	32

✂ FROM WELSH DRAGON TO ROVER ✂

In September 2004, Mark Hughes resigned as the manager of the Welsh national side to take up his new appointment as manager of Blackburn Rovers. Hughes, nicknamed "Sparky", succeeded Graeme Souness, who became manager of Newcastle United.

✂ POWER SWITCH IN LONDON ✂

When Chelsea retained the Premier League title in the 2005–06 season, Arsenal, who had the Premiership crown three times, were a distant 24 points behind their London rivals in fourth place. It was the first time Arsene Wenger's team had finished outside the top three since he took charge of the Gunners in 1996.

✂ TIGANA WALKS ✂

In March 2003 Jean Tigana left his position as manager of Fulham and was succeeded by club captain Chris Coleman.

❧ THE TINKER MAN TAKES CHARGE ❧

In September 2000, Chelsea sacked their Italian manager Gianluca Vialli and replaced him with another Italian, Claudio Ranieri. During his time in charge at Stamford Bridge Ranieri was dubbed the "Tinker Man" by the British press on account of the number of times he changed his starting line-up.

❧ BREACH OF CONTRACT SACKING ❧

On 16 March 2001, Tottenham Hotspur sacked manager George Graham for what the club claimed was a breach of contract. Two weeks later, Spurs' former golden boy, Glenn Hoddle, returned to White Hart Lane from Southampton as their new manager and made another former Spurs favourite, Teddy Sheringham, his first purchase. However, Hoddle's departure from the Saints went down badly with the club's fans.

❧ BANK BUSTERS ❧

In late January 1995, Manchester United set a new British transfer record when they signed Andy Cole from Newcastle United for £7 million (£6 million plus the £1m-rated Keith Gillespie).

❧ A REAL DOG-FIGHT ❧

In each of the last three weekends of the 2004–05 Premier League season the team that was sitting bottom of the Premiership table at the start of the weekend finished it outside the drop zone.

❧ OVER THE HALF ❧

Manchester United's David Beckham scored a goal from his own half against Wimbledon at Selhurst Park on the opening day of the 1996–97 season. His speculative shot sailed 55 yards and over the head of the Dons' keeper Neil Sullivan.

❧ EAGLES SWOOP INTO DIVISION ONE ❧

Crystal Palace ended season 1992–93 with 49 points from 42 Premiership games and were relegated on goal difference. Their points tally equalled the highest of any club ever to be relegated from the top flight of English football.

⚜ 2012–13 PREMIER LEAGUE CLUB MASCOTS ⚜

❖ Baggie Bird – West Bromwich Albion ❖
❖ Billy the Badger/Terry Bytes – Fulham ❖
❖ Bubbles the Bear/Herbie the Hammer – West Ham United ❖
❖ Camilla Canary and Captain Canary – Norwich City ❖
❖ Chirpy Cockerel – Tottenham Hotspur ❖
❖ Cyril and Cybil the Swans – Swansea City ❖
❖ Fred the Red – Manchester United ❖
❖ Gunnersaurus Rex – Arsenal ❖
❖ Hercules the Lion – Aston Villa ❖
❖ JJ and B – Wigan Athletic ❖
❖ Jude The Cat – Queens Park Rangers ❖
❖ Kingsley Royal (lion) – Reading ❖
❖ Monty Magpie – Newcastle United ❖
❖ Moonchester (space alien) – Manchester City ❖
❖ Mr Toffee – Everton ❖
❖ Pottermus Hippo and Pottermiss Hippo – Stoke City ❖
❖ Samson and Delilah (black cats) – Sunderland ❖
❖ Stamford Lion – Chelsea ❖
❖ Super Saint – Southampton ❖

Did You Know That?
Liverpool don't have a mascot.

⚜ AN AMAZING TURNAROUND ⚜

Micky Adams, who played for Southampton in the Premiership during the 1993–94 season, guided Fulham into Division Two at the end of the 1996–97 season. Amazingly, just 18 months earlier, the London club lay in 23rd place in Division Three, 91st (out of 92 league clubs) in the whole Football League.

⚜ A HAT-TRICK OF HAMMERINGS ⚜

Over the space of nine days in March 2008, West Ham United suffered three consecutive 4–0 defeats in the Premier League. The tale of misery went as follows:

Date	Opponents	Venue
1 March	Chelsea	Upton Park
5 March	Liverpool	Anfield
9 March	Tottenham Hotspur	White Hart Lane

✂ FULL HOUSE AT THE THEATRE OF DREAMS ✂

Manchester United's 4–1 hammering of Lancashire rivals Blackburn Rovers at Old Trafford en route to winning the 2007 Premier League title was attended by a crowd of 76,098. The bumper crowd is United's all-time record home attendance and it is also the highest-ever attendance for a Premiership game. Given that Old Trafford's capacity is 16,000 more than any other club in Premier League history, it is no surprise that Manchester United have all of the Top 100 home attendances recorded for a Premier League game.

✂ THE NORTH-WEST INFLUENCE ✂

Eight of the 20 Premier League clubs in 2009–10 were from the north-west: Blackburn Rovers, Bolton Wanderers, Burnley, Everton, Liverpool, Manchester City, Manchester United and Wigan Athletic. By 2013–14, only Everton, Liverpool, City and United remained.

✂ THIRD TIME LUCKY ✂

After two successive Wembley defeats for Leicester City in the Division One play-off final, Brian Little finally guided them into the FA Premier League for season 1994–95 when the Foxes beat Derby 2–1 the play-off final. They were joined in the top flight by Crystal Palace, First Division champions in 1993–94, and runners-up Nottingham Forest.

✂ A ROYAL SEASON ✂

The 2006–07 season saw Reading playing in the top flight for the first time in their 135-year history. The Royals got off to a good start too, winning their inaugural Premiership game against Middlesbrough 3–2.

✂ BLUES FOR THE BLUE & WHITES ✂

In the 2012–13 season, wearing solid coloured shirts seemed to be a better option. Only Arsenal, with white sleeves to go with their red shirts, finished in the top seven, but it was a different story at the other end of the table. The three relegated teams, Queens Park Rangers, Reading and Wigan Athletic, all wore blue and white – the Wigan striped, the other two hooped – and four of the five above them, Stoke City, Southampton, Sunderland and Newcastle United all sported stripes, while Aston Villa's colours are claret with sky blue sleeves.

❧ PREMIERSHIP TALK (21) ❧

"It's getting tickly now – squeaky-bum time, I call it."
Sir Alex Ferguson on the 2002–03 end-of-season title race won by United

❧ EVERTON TIGERS ❧

In season 2007–08 Everton FC entered a team in the British Basketball League, the Everton Tigers.

❧ BORO LAND MACCARONE ❧

Prior to the start of the 2002–03 season Middlesbrough broke the club record transfer fee by paying £8.15 million for the services of the Italian international striker Massimo Maccarone from Empoli. The 21-year-old had made the front pages of the Italain newspapers in March 2002 when he became the first Serie B player to be selected for the Italian national side in 20 years. In his first season at The Riverside he scored nine times, but he never really settled in Middlesbrough. During season 2004–05 he was loaned out to Parma in Serie A before returning to Boro for the start of the 2005–06 Premiership campaign. He joined the Italian club Siena in early 2007 on a free transfer.

❧ TROPHYLESS GUNNERS ❧

On 12 May 2001 Arsenal faced Liverpool in the FA Cup final, the first to be played at the Millennium Stadium, Cardiff, while Wembley Stadium was being rebuilt. The Gunners took the lead in the game and looked likely to end the season with their first piece of silverware in three seasons only to see Michael Owen score two goals in the last five minutes and hand the FA Cup to the Anfield club. Going into the game Arsenal had just finished runners-up to Manchester United in the Premier League for the third season on the trot.

❧ MAGPIES SEEING DOUBLE ❧

Newcastle United ended the 1996–97 season in exactly the same spot where they ended the previous season, runners-up to Manchester United. However, this time the Geordies trailed seven points behind United, three more than had been the case the last campaign.

❧ TRACTOR BOYS MOWED DOWN ❧

The 1994–95 season was one of the worst in Ipswich Town's history. The Tractor Boys conceded 92 Premiership goals and managed a meagre seven wins all season (in 42 league games plus the League Cup and FA Cup). Their 29 Premiership defeats including a humiliating 9–0 loss at Manchester United.

❧ A UNIQUE DOUBLE ❧

Mark Walters was the first player to score for Liverpool in the Premier League, on 19 August 1992 against Sheffield United at Anfield, and also the first to score a hat-trick for Liverpool in the Premier League, on 17 April 1993 against Coventry City at Anfield.

❧ AN OLD VILLAN RETURNS TO THE PARK ❧

On 24 January 2002, John Gregory resigned as manager of Aston Villa after four years in charge. He was replaced by the former England manager Graham Taylor, who had previously guided Aston Villa into the First Division in 1987–88 and to a championship runners-up spot in 1989–90. This success with Aston Villa, plus his earlier work at Watford, prompted the Football Association to come looking for Taylor's services, and he was appointed England manager after Bobby Robson stepped down from the role following the 1990 World Cup finals. Villa ended 2001–02 eighth in the Premiership table – their tenth consecutive top-ten finish.

❧ UNITED GIVE ROVERS EUROPEAN BERTH ❧

Manchester United's second-place finish behind Chelsea in the 2005–06 Premier League (guaranteeing them UEFA Champions League football in 2006–07) added to their League Cup success (a 4–0 win over Premiership new boys Wigan Athletic at the Millennium Stadium, Cardiff) meant that the Red Devils' place in the UEFA Cup went to the team that finished sixth in the Premier League table, Blackburn Rovers.

❧ LEAKY LEEDS GOAL DROUGHT ❧

In 1996–97 George Graham's Leeds United scored fewer goals than any other Premier League side (28) yet still managed to end the season in a secure 11th position. They conceded 38 goals.

⅍ ALAN SHEARER, OBE ⅋

Alan Shearer was born in Newcastle-upon-Tyne on 13 August 1970. At the age of 16, while playing as a schoolboy at the famous Wallsend Boys Club, the young striker was rejected by Newcastle United and instead signed as an apprentice for Southampton. On 26 March 1988 he made his first-team debut as a substitute against Chelsea and, a fortnight later, in his first start, scored a hat-trick against Arsenal. At 17 years and 8 months, he became the youngest player ever to score a hat-trick in top-flight English football, breaking Jimmy Greaves' 30-year-old record.

On 19 February 1992, Shearer won his first full England cap and he scored on his international debut against France at Wembley in a 2–0 win. He was a member of the England squad that qualified for that year's European Championships in Sweden, making one appearance at the finals. Alan was, however, the obvious replacement for the retiring Gary Lineker. In 1992 he left the Saints and signed for Blackburn Rovers for a £3.6 million transfer fee, a British record. It was at Ewood Park that he won his only major club honour in the game, the FA Premier League title in season 1994–95. He was voted the PFA Player of the Year for 1994–95 and received the same award from his peers two years later.

Alan won the 1996 European Championships' Golden Boot award with five goals. Later that summer, Newcastle paid a world record £15 million to Blackburn Rovers to secure his services. Alan helped England to qualify for the 1998 World Cup finals and, in 1999, Kevin Keegan made him captain. Shearer was an ever-present as England reached the 2000 European Championships. In the finals Alan headed the winner against Germany, but England were knocked out at the group stage. He scored his 30th England goal against Romania that night, in his 63rd appearance, but retired from international football after England's exit.

On 18 January 2003, Alan scored after only ten seconds for Newcastle United against Manchester City, the joint-fastest goal in Premier League history and joint-fastest scored by a Newcastle player, matching Jackie Milburn in November 1947. In January 2006, he scored his 200th goal for Newcastle to break Milburn's club record. Alan retired at the end of the 2005–06 season, having notched up 206 goals for the Magpies and a Premier League record of 261. On 1 April 2009, Alan moved out of the TV pundit's chair – where he had been since retiring – to take over the managerial hot-seat at St James' Park. He had eight games to save Newcastle but couldn't do it, and resigned after the Magpies' relegation. Alan returned to his highly-successful position as a fototbal pundit.

Did You Know That?
Alan had a cameo role in the 2005 movie, *Goal!*

❧ BACK UP WHERE THEY BELONG ❧

Manchester United's 4–0 win over Wigan Athletic at Old Trafford on 6 October 2007 sent the Red Devils to the top of the Premiership table for the first time since they won the Premiership crown at the end of the 2006–07 season.

❧ AL THE FOURTEENTH ❧

When Alan Shearer was signed from Blackburn Rovers for a world-record transfer fee of £15 million in July 1996, he was Kevin Keegan's 14th and last eight-figure purchase for the club during his first spell in charge of the Magpies (1992–97).

❧ DOPEY STRIKER ❧

In February 1995, Crystal Palace striker Chris Armstrong failed a random drugs test, having tested positive for cannabis. Armstrong had no hesitation in openly admitting he had done wrong and agreed to undergo a rehabilitation programme.

❧ REBROV DOWN THE LANE ❧

When Tottenham Hotspur finished the 1999–2000 season in a disappointing tenth place, they decided to bolster their attack for the 2000–01 season and shelled out a club record £11 million for FC Dynamo Kiev's Ukrainian international striker Sergi Rebrov. Rebrov had just ended the 1999–2000 season as the joint top scorer in the UEFA Champions League with ten goals. Following the sacking of George Graham as Spurs manager in March 2001 Rebrov failed to earn a regular starting place in the team under new boss Glenn Hoddle and over the next few seasons went out on two consecutive loan spells with Turkish club Fenerbahce, before signing a one-year contract with West Ham United in 2004. During his time at Kiev he won the Ukrainian Premier League nine times, the Ukrainian Cup seven times and the Ukrainian Super Cup and, in 2003–04, he won the Turkish league championship with Fenerbahce.

❧ CRAZY GANG ON THE MOVE ❧

On 21 June 2004, former Premiership club Wimbledon announced that they would be moving away from South London to Milton Keynes and changing their name to the Milton Keynes Dons.

♕ FINAL PREMIERSHIP TABLE 2005–2006 ♕

Pos	Team	P	W	D	L	F	A	Pts
1.	Chelsea (C)	38	29	4	5	72	22	91
2.	Manchester United	38	25	8	5	72	34	83
3.	Liverpool	38	25	7	6	57	25	82
4.	Arsenal	38	20	7	11	68	31	67
5.	Tottenham Hotspur	38	18	11	9	53	38	65
6.	Blackburn Rovers	38	19	6	13	51	42	63
7.	Newcastle United	38	17	7	14	47	42	58
8.	Bolton Wanderers	38	15	11	12	49	41	56
9.	West Ham United	38	16	7	15	52	55	55
10.	Wigan Athletic	38	15	6	17	45	52	51
11.	Everton	38	14	8	16	34	49	50
12.	Fulham	38	14	6	18	48	58	48
13.	Charlton Athletic	38	13	8	17	41	55	47
14.	Middlesbrough	38	12	9	17	48	58	45
15.	Manchester City	38	13	4	21	43	48	43
16.	Aston Villa	38	10	12	16	42	55	42
17.	Portsmouth	38	10	8	20	37	62	38
18.	Birmingham City (R)	38	8	10	20	28	50	34
19.	West Bromwich Albion (R)	38	7	9	22	31	58	30
20.	Sunderland (R)	38	3	6	29	26	69	15

♕ A 39TH GAME WAS NEARLY A REALITY ♕

Sorting out the final places at the end of the 2012–13 Premiership season was nearly decided by a playoff. Going into the final round of matches, Chelsea (third, hosting Everton) were two points ahead of Arsenal (fourth, away to Newcastle United) and three of Tottenham Hotspur (fifth, at home to Sunderland). If the Blues had drawn 0–0 and the Gunners won 4–2, they would have been on 73 points each, a +35 goal difference, with 75 scored and 39 conceded. However, in the unlikely event of a 9–0 Spurs win and 7–0 Chelsea loss, these two clubs would also have had absolutely identical points and goals. As it was all three clubs won 1–0, so the final order was Chelsea, Arsenal, Tottenham.

♕ FOUR GAMES AND OUT ♕

Peter Reid was sacked by Manchester City after just four games of the 1993–94 Premiership campaign, and Oxford United manager Brian Horton became the new boss at Maine Road. The Citizens had lost their opening four fixtures.

❧ PREMIERSHIP TALK (22) ❧

"They say he's an intelligent man, right? Speaks five languages! I've got a 15-year-old boy from the Ivory Coast who speaks five languages!"
Sir Alex Ferguson on his nemesis Arsene Wenger

❧ CHASING LIVERPOOL ❧

Manchester United won their tenth FA Premier League title in the 2007–08 season to make it 17 top-flight championship titles, second only to Liverpool's record of 18 titles.

❧ BARCLAYCARD ANYONE? ❧

The Premiership's tenth season in 2001–02 attracted a new sponsor and became known as the Barclaycard Premier League.

❧ CRESTFALLEN CHAMPIONS ❧

In late October 1996 Blackburn Rovers, Premiership Champions 18 months previously, found themselves bottom of the Premier League table. Following the resignation of manager Ray Harford, Tony Parkes took charge until the end of the season and helped Rovers avoid the drop with a 13th-place finish.

❧ BOXING DAY SPOILER ❧

On Boxing Day 2002, Darren Ambrose scored in the last minute for Ipswich Town in their Premiership encounter with Leicester City. A year later, on Boxing Day 2003, Ambrose was the scourge of Leicester City once again, this time hitting a last-minute winner against them for Newcastle United.

❧ SUPER RONNY ❧

The 2006–07 PFA Players' Player of the Year Award was won by Manchester United's Cristiano Ronaldo. The Portuguese star also scooped the PFA Young Player of the Year Award, making him the first player to win both prestigious awards since Everton's Andy Gray in 1977, who was the only player to have done it before. By picking up the Young Player Award Ronaldo prevented his United team-mate Wayne Rooney from collecting it for a third consecutive year.

✂ CLEAN SHEET KING ✂

David James enjoyed a long and successful career in England's top tier, a run which came to an end with Portsmouth's relegation in 2010. Now into his 40s and still playing – he was at Bournemouth in 2012–13 and ended the season less than 25 matches short of 1,000 in senior football – James holds the Premier League record for most clean sheets with 173.

✂ ROONEY AND GERRARD SHARE AWARDS ✂

Wayne Rooney and Steven Gerrard share the record for having won the most Premier League Player of the Month awards – five each.

✂ LONG EXILES ✂

At the end of the 1998–99 season none of the three sides relegated from the Premiership the previous season regained their top-division status. However, Sunderland returned to the Premiership after a two-year exile by virtue of winning the First Division championship and were joined in the top flight by Bradford City and play-off winners Watford. Watford had endured an 11-year exile from the top flight, whereas Bradford City's exile had lasted 11 times longer, 77 years.

✂ A RUUD APPOINTMENT ✂

When Glenn Hoddle decided to vacate his position as Chelsea manager at the end of the 1995–96 season and take-up his new post as England manager, the Blues acted swiftly and appointed their 33-year-old Dutch superstar Ruud Gullit as player-manager. The Dutch maestro immediately went for the Stamford Bridge chequebook and forked out a club record £4.9 million for the Italian midfielder Roberto Di Matteo.

✂ FOUR SAFE HANDS ✂

In season 2002–03, Chelsea goalkeeper Carlo Cudicini won the inaugural Barclaycard Golden Gloves Award after keeping 12 clean sheets (the most by any goalkeeper during the season) and only conceding 35 goals. However, the No.1 shirt in the inaugural 2002–03 PFA Team of the Year went to Blackburn Rovers goalkeeper Brad Friedel.

❧ FOOTBALL SEARCHING FOR LOST SOUL ❧

In an interview with the *Daily Telegraph* on 6 October 2007, Sunderland manager Roy Keane spoke very frankly about the state of football: "Football has lost its soul and it's definitely for the worse. It is not the game I knew ten years ago. It's changing and it's sad. There are lots of things like kick-off times, small things that make a difference. Clubs are being sold and fans are complaining about prices. I know [Manchester] United fans were complaining last week about having to buy tickets for the Coventry match. Every club is changing, and not always for the good. The day I left the club I had been involved with for a long, long time [United], it was different to the one I joined. That's why I don't really miss playing. United against Arsenal – if you could go back for one game, it would be that. If I was playing Arsenal on the Saturday, my preparation would start on the previous Sunday. Psychologically, you would prepare."

❧ THE ACADEMY ❧

In 2000 Liverpool took the decision to fund and build a multimillion-pound football academy in order to continue nurturing and developing their own young talent. This world-class facility, situated at Kirkby and under the expert guidance of academy director and Liverpool legend Steve Heighway, is designed to give every young boy on the club's books the best possible chance of emulating past products of the Liverpool youth system, such as Robbie Fowler, Steve McManaman, Jamie Carragher, Michael Owen and Steven Gerrard.

❧ SPURS DENY UNITED THE QUADRUPLE ❧

Manchester United were knocked out of the 1998–99 League Cup by the eventual winners Tottenham Hotspur. It proved to be the only competition United failed to win that season. Otherwise they swept all before them, winning the Premier League, FA Cup and UEFA Champions League.

❧ A RETURN TO WINNING WAYS ❧

In 1997–98, his second season in charge of Leeds United, George Graham guided Leeds United, helped by 16 Premiership goals from Jimmy Floyd Hasselbaink, to an eventual fifth place in the Premiership and guaranteed UEFA Cup football for the following season.

❧ PREMIERSHIP TALK (23) ❧

"If he was an inch taller he'd be the best centre-half in Britain. His father is six foot two – I'd check the milkman."
Sir Alex Ferguson on *Gary Neville*

❧ A MUTUAL PARTING ❧

On 17 October 2007, Bolton Wanderers announced that the club had parted company with manager Sammy Lee by "mutual consent". Lee had only been in the post for six months having taken over the helm from Sam Allardyce in April 2007 after Big Sam moved to Newcastle United. However, things had not gone well for Lee at the Reebok Stadium, and at the time of his departure the club was lying second from bottom of the Premiership, with only one league win in the season so far. It was widely believed that Lee's departure may have been hastened by his falling-out with Gary Speed the previous week.

❧ PREMATURE PAY OUT ❧

During the 1997–98 season Manchester United looked on course for a fifth Premiership title as they led the league by 11 points going into March. One turf accountant even paid out on bets placed for United to win the title. However, Arsenal put in a fine run of late season form, including a 1–0 win over United at Old Trafford on 14 March 1998 (cutting United's lead to six points with three games in hand), and pipped United for the crown by a single point.

❧ SUPER TED ❧

Teddy Sheringham scored 14 times for Spurs in the Premiership during the 1993–94 season even though restricted by injury to making only 19 appearances for the London club.

❧ THE SAINTLY SINNER ❧

When Glenn Hoddle resigned as Southampton manager in late March 2001 to take over at Tottenham Hotspur, the Saints turned to Stuart Gray, whose temporary appointment was made permanent thanks to the club's good run of form under his stewardship. Southampton finished the 2000–01 season in 10th place in the Premier League, a satisfying two places above Hoddle's Spurs.

❧ DUTCH PREMIER LEAGUE FANTASY XI ❧

1
Edwin
Van der SAR
(MANCHESTER UTD)

2
Giovanni
Van BRONCKHORST
(ARSENAL)

5
Mario
MELCHIOT
(ASTON VILLA)

6
Jaap
STAM
(MANCHESTER UTD)

3
Wilfred
BOUMA
(ASTON VILLA)

4
Ruud
GULLIT
(CHELSEA, CAPT)

7
Rafael
VAN DER VAART
(TOTTENHAM HOTSPUR)

8
Robin
Van PERSIE
(MANCHESTER UNITED)

9
Ruud
Van NISTELROOY
(MANCHESTER UTD)

10
Dennis
BERGKAMP
(ARSENAL)

11
Marc
OVERMARS
(ARSENAL)

Substitutes

Ed de *GOEIJ (Chelsea)* • Andre *OOIJER (Blackburn)* • John *HEITINGER (Everton)* •
Denny *LANDZAAT (Wigan Athletic)* • Dirk *KUYT (Liverpool)*
Edgar *DAVIDS (Tottenanham Hotspur)* Arjen *ROBBEN (Chelsea)*

Manager

Martin *JOL (Fulham)*

Did You Know That?
Martin Jol was capped three times by the Netherlands.

❧ UNLUCKY 13 FOR REDS IN 200TH DERBY ❧

The Merseyside derby has been the most frequently played derby match in English football history. The 200th Merseyside derby was played at Goodison Park on 11 December 2004 in front of 40,552 fans. It was the 99th meeting at Goodison and the 25th time the two sides had met in the Premier League. But Liverpool's 13th away Premiership derby against Everton proved unlucky as the Toffees won the game 1–0 with a Lee Carsley goal in the 68th minute.

❧ LACK-LUSTRE VILLANS ❧

Aston Villa finished the 2002–03 season 16th in the Premiership, just two places and three points clear of relegation. Villa only managed 12 league wins during the campaign, 11 of them coming at Villa Park.

⚜ WHEN THE RED MIST DESCENDS ⚜

Despite playing in only 18 of the Premier League's 21 seasons, Blackburn Rovers' players have been the most ill-disciplined with 76 red cards being shown to them. In fact three of the "top" six bad boys have not been Premiership ever-presents:

Pos	Club	Seasons	Red Cards	Average
1.	Blackburn Rovers	18	75	4.17
2.	Everton	21	74	3.52
3.	Arsenal	21	69	3.29
4.	Chelsea	21	64	3.05
5.	Newcastle United	19	62	3.26
6.	West Ham United	17	60	3.53

⚜ A MYSTERIOUS DEPARTURE ⚜

On 9 May 2001, Harry Redknapp stepped down as manager of West Ham United after seven years in charge. His sudden departure from the Upton Park club, which had finished 15th in the Premiership table, was totally unexpected and remained a mystery. The Hammers appointed first-team coach Glenn Roeder as Redknapp's successor.

⚜ LATICS HAND TITLE TO UNITED ⚜

When Oldham Athletic produced a shock 1–0 win over Aston Villa at Villa Park towards the end of the 1992–93 season, the inaugural Premier League title went to Manchester United.

⚜ OCEANIA FOOTBALLER OF THE YEAR ⚜

The Oceania Footballer of the Year Award is chosen by a forum of southern-hemisphere journalists and is presented to the best footballer from the Oceania region. Australian Harry Kewell, of Liverpool, won it in 2003, having also won it in 1999 when he was at Leeds United. Kewell is the only Liverpool player to have won the award.

⚜ NO TURKISH DELIGHT IN EUROPE ⚜

During the 1996–97 season, Manchester United lost their 40-year unbeaten home record in Europe. The first team to beat United at Old Trafford was Fenerbahce of Turkey, who won a UEFA Champions League Group C match 1–0. United still reached the quarter-finals.

⚜ ALL CHANGE AMONG THE OWLS ⚜

Sheffield Wednesday sacked manager Danny Wilson in March 2000 and replaced him with his assistant Peter Shreeves. Shreeves took charge of the Owls until the end of the season, but could not save them from relegation. At the end of the season Paul Jewell (who, ironically, had helped Bradford City avoid the drop from the Premiership in 1999–2000) walked out of Valley Parade to take charge of the Hillsborough club, with Shreeves reverting to his assistant's position. Meanwhile, Bradford City appointed Jewell's assistant, Chris Hutchings, as their new manager.

⚜ ROCKET MEN GO DOWN ⚜

Watford set an unwanted Premier League record in 1999–2000. They finished bottom of the table with just 24 points, the lowest number in Premiership history (a record subsequently broken on two occasions, most recently by 11-point Derby County in 2007–08). Of the three clubs promoted to the Premiership at the start of the season, Watford was the only one to be relegated – both Bradford City and Sunderland survived at the expense of Sheffield Wednesday and Wimbledon.

⚜ ALL WRIGHT ⚜

Ian Wright is the only player to have been the Golden Boot winner (top goalscorer) in both the old First Division and the Premier League. He headed the list with 29 goals in 1991–92, the last season of the old First Division, and in the Premier League with 24 goals in 1996–97.

⚜ FOXES NO LONGER IN THE HUNT ⚜

At the end of September 2001, Leicester City sacked manager Peter Taylor and replaced him with Dave Bassett following a disappointing start to the season. Mickey Adams was brought in as Bassett's assistant. However, the Foxes were unable to stop the slide into Division One and were relegated after losing 1–0 at home to Manchester United on 6 April 2002. Leicester City finished bottom of the Premiership table with just 28 points from their 38 Premiership games. Prior to their relegation, Bassett moved upstairs at Filbert Street to become the club's director of football, and Adams was promoted to the manager's seat, with former Cardiff City manager Alan Cork being named as Adams' assistant.

❧ FINAL PREMIERSHIP TABLE 2006–2007 ❧

Pos	Team	P	W	D	L	F	A	Pts
1.	Manchester United (C)	38	28	5	5	83	27	89
2.	Chelsea	38	24	11	3	64	24	83
3.	Liverpool	38	20	8	10	57	27	68
4.	Arsenal	38	19	11	8	63	35	68
5.	Tottenham Hotspur	38	17	9	12	57	54	60
6.	Everton	38	15	13	10	52	36	58
7.	Bolton Wanderers	38	16	8	14	47	52	56
8.	Reading	38	16	7	15	52	47	55
9.	Portsmouth	38	14	12	12	45	42	54
10.	Blackburn Rovers	38	15	7	16	52	54	52
11.	Aston Villa	38	11	17	10	43	41	50
12.	Middlesbrough	38	12	10	16	44	49	46
13.	Newcastle United	38	11	10	17	38	47	43
14.	Manchester City	38	11	9	18	29	44	42
15.	West Ham United	38	12	5	21	35	59	41
16.	Fulham	38	8	15	15	38	60	39
17.	Wigan Athletic	38	10	8	20	37	59	38
18.	Sheffield United (R)	38	10	8	20	32	55	38
19.	Charlton Athletic (R)	38	8	10	20	34	60	34
20.	Watford (R)	38	5	13	20	29	59	28

❧ GOAL-LINE TECHNOLOGY COMES IN ❧

The 2013–14 Premier League season will go down in the history books as the first when goal-line techology was used to decide goals. Ever since the 1966 World Cup final when England's third goal against West Germany was given, but a potential equaliser in the 2010 second round not, these have been contentious issues. FIFA, after a U-turn in 2008, finally bowed to the pressure and allowed football associations to trial the technology. Two systems were looked at Hawk-Eye, used in cricket and tennis, and Goal Control, and the Premier League opted to go with the former system, but only for goal/no goal decisions.

❧ LEADING ALL THE WAY ❧

On 23 August 1993, Manchester United beat Aston Villa, Premiership runners-up to United in the previous season, 2–1 at Villa Park to move to top place in the Premiership table. Amazingly, United stayed there for the rest of the season and, eight months later, were crowned champions for the second successive year.

SIR TREVOR STEPS INTO THE BREACH

In April 2003, West Ham manager Glenn Roeder was forced to stand down temporarily when he after being diagnosed with a brain tumour. Former West Ham legend Sir Trevor Brooking took charge until Glenn was fit enough to return. However, not even Brooking could prevent West Ham from being relegated after they finished 18th in the Premiership table that season. Sunderland, who finished bottom and West Bromwich Albion, 19th, also went down with the Hammers.

PREMIERSHIP TALK (24)

"At a young age winning is not the most important thing... the important thing is to develop creative and skilled players with good confidence."
Arsenal manager ***Arsene Wenger***

WE'LL BE BACK

After they were relegated to Division One at the end of the 1993–94 season, John Gorman the manager of Swindon Town said that the Robins "won't be in Division One for long". Gorman was right: the Robins went on a downward spiral, including relegation to League Two (England's fourth tier) in 2006.

YOUNG MICHAEL OWEN

Liverpool's 18-year-old striker Michael Owen scored 18 Premier League goals in 36 games in the 1997–98 season, helping Liverpool to third place in the table and UEFA Cup football for season 1998–99. Owen's 18 goals made him the Premiership's joint top goalscorer and won him both the PFA Young Player of the Year Award and the Carling Player of the Year Award, as well as place in Glenn Hoddle's England 1998 World Cup finals squad.

CANARIES FALL OUT OF THE NEST

Norwich City finished third in the inaugural Premiership table in 1992–93. Two years later they finished 20th and were relegated after spending nine years in the top flight. From the start of the season to the beginning of the following season they had three managers: John Deehan, Gary Megson (player-manager) and Martin O'Neill.

❧ TEVEZ DOES IT AGAIN ❧

Carlos Tevez scored and collected win bonuses in Manchester United's final home game of the season in both 2006–07 and 2007–08. In the first of these, he was playing for West Ham United as they won 1–0 at Old Trafford. Twelve months later, coincidentally also against the Hammers, he was on target for the home team as they won 4–1.

❧ THE £100M MAN ❧

In his four years in charge of Leeds United (1998–99 to 2001–02) David O'Leary spent £100 million in the transfer market, but failed to bring any silverware to Elland Road.

❧ OCTUPUS TURNS INTO A MAGPIE ❧

In early 1996 Kevin Keegan brought the Colombian international Faustino Hernan Asprilla Hinestroza to Newcastle United from Parma. Asprilla had two nicknames, "The Octopus" and "Two-Goal Tino", the former on account of his flexible style of play and the latter because he usually scored for his teams in twos.

❧ THAT SINKING FEELING ❧

Nottingham Forest suffered their third relegation from the Premier League in seven seasons at the end of the 1998–99 season; they had also gone down in 1992–93 and 1996–97. Forest finished bottom of the table while Blackburn Rovers, Premiership champions in 1994–95, also went down along with Charlton Athletic.

❧ THERE'S ONLY TWO KEANOS ❧

During the 1999–2000 season Robbie Keane scored 12 goals in 34 Premier League appearances for Coventry City. Meanwhile the other R. Keane, Roy, captained Manchester United to the Premier League title.

❧ BE GONE ❧

Seven Premier League clubs have started with the letter "B", but following Bolton's and Blackburn's relegation at the end of the 2011–12 season, none remained. That said, Barnsley, Blackpool and Burnley lasted only one season each and Bradford City just two.

❧ EAGLES SWOOP BEFORE FALLING ❧

In 1995 newly promoted Crystal Palace reached the semi-finals of both the FA Cup and League Cup competitions, but their excellent domestic Cup form did not carry over into their Premiership, as they made an instant return to the First Division. In a strange twist of fate the Eagles finished in the last four of all the competitions they entered in 1994–95, but that season, unfortunately, last four in the Premiership meant relegation.

❧ THE MAN OF MANY TONGUES ❧

Arsene Wenger, the manager of Arsenal, is fluent in French, Alsatian, English and German and also speaks Italian, Japanese and Spanish.

❧ CUP-LOSERS GET CUP WINNERS' CUP SPOT ❧

Manchester United beat Liverpool in the 1996 FA Cup final thanks to a late goal from their French talisman Eric Cantona. The win gave United the Double for the second time in the club's history. Their Premiership success meant that United would play in the Champions League in 1996–97, while Liverpool would take their place in the European Cup Winners' Cup.

❧ A HISTORIC SEASON ❧

The 2001–02 Premiership season was notable for the fact that it was the first time in the competition's history that all three promoted teams avoided relegation – Blackburn Rovers (finished tenth), Fulham (13th) and Bolton Wanderers (16th).

❧ UNITED'S DOZEN ❧

In season 1998–99 Manchester United won their fifth Premier League title in seven years, their 12th Championship success.

❧ PREMIERSHIP TALK (25) ❧

"If you have no eggs, you have no omelette. And it also depends on the quality of the eggs. In the supermarket you have class one eggs, and you also have class two and class three. Some are more expensive than others and they give you better omelettes."
Former Chelsea manager Jose Mourinho

❧ FRENCH PREMIER LEAGUE FANTASY XI ❧

1
Fabien
BARTHEZ
(MANCHESTER UTD)

2
Mikael
SILVESTRE
(MANCHESTER UTD & ARSENAL)

6
Laurent
BLANC
(MANCHESTER UTD)

5
William
GALLAS
(CHELSEA, ARSENAL & SPURS)

3
Patrice
EVRA
(MANCHESTER UTD)

7
Eric
CANTONA
(LEEDS UTD & MAN UTD, CAPT.)

4
Patrick
VIEIRA
(ARSENAL & MAN CITY)

8
Claude
MAKELELE
(CHELSEA)

9
Nicolas
ANELKA
(CHELSEA et al)

10
Thierry
HENRY
(ARSENAL)

11
Robert
PIRES
(ARSENAL, WEST HAM & ASTON VILLA)

Substitutes

Lionel *PEREZ (Sunderland)* • Abou *DIABY (Arsenal)* • Gael *CLICHY (Arsenal)* •
Samir *NASRI (Arsenal & Manchester City)* • Florent *MALOUDA (Chelsea)* •
David *GINOLA (Newcastle Utd & Tottenham)* • Louis *SAHA (Manchester Utd)*

Manager

Arsene *WENGER* OBE *(Arsenal)*

Did You Know That?

Claude Makelele was born in Kinshasa, Zaire (now the Democratic Republic of the Congo) and Patrice Evra was born in Dakar, Senegal.

❧ LIVERPOOL BACK IN EUROPE ❧

Liverpool finished third in the Premiership in season 2000–01, 11 points behind champions Manchester United, and qualified for the 2001–02 UEFA Champions League. Liverpool had not participated in Europe's premier club competition since the fateful 1985 final at Heysel, where 39 Juventus fans were killed. After the 1985 European Cup final, in which Juventus beat Liverpool 1–0, UEFA banned all English clubs from European football for six years.

❧ ADDICKS ON THE RISE ❧

Charlton Athletic finished ninth in the Premiership in the 2000–01 season, the Addicks' highest league position since the 1950s.

☙ FOLLOWING THE SPECIAL ONE ❧

When Jose Mourinho left Chelsea on 20 September 2007, he was replaced by Chelsea's director of football, Avram Grant, just 74 days after he arrived at Stamford Bridge. Grant had previously coached in Israel, at Maccabi Tel Aviv (1991–95 & 1997–2000) and Maccabi Haifa (2000–02). He led Maccabi Tel Aviv to the Liga Leumit (Israeli championship) in 1992 and 1995 and to Israeli Cup success in 1994 and guided Maccabi Haifa to Liga Leumit titles in 2001 and 2002. In May 2002 he was appointed the national coach of Israel and almost steered them to the 2006 World Cup finals. Despite being unbeaten in their group (W4, D6) they finished third behind France and Switzerland. In June 2006, Portsmouth appointed him as their technical director and on 8 July 2007 Roman Abramovich brought him to Chelsea. "Avram is here to help," said Jose Mourinho, speaking on Chelsea's pre-season 2007 tour of the USA. "He does not want to create problems for people."

☙ A BRIEF STAY ❧

Bolton Wanderers (Division One champions in 1996–97), Barnsley (runners-up) and Crystal Palace (play-off final winners) were all promoted to the Premiership for the 1997–98 season. At the end of the season all three newly promoted teams dropped back into Division One.

☙ BAD TRAVELLERS ❧

Leeds United, winners of the last-ever Division One championship in 1991–92, failed to win any of their 21 away games during the inaugural FA Premier League season in 1992–93. Their final league position was 17th, three places above a relegation berth. It marked a huge fall from grace.

☙ A MAN FOR ALL LEAGUES ❧

Steve Finnan is the only player to have played in the Premier League, League Divisions One, Two and Three, the Football Conference, the League Cup, the FA Cup, the UEFA Cup, the UEFA Champions League and the FIFA World Cup finals. The Irish international achieved this feat with Welling United (1993–95), Birmingham City (1995–96), Notts County (1996–98), Fulham (1998–2003) and Liverpool (2003–08).

❧ ALL WHITE, ALL WRONG ❧

Following the Premiership games over the weekend of 20–21 October 2007, the three teams lying at the foot of the Premiership table all had white jerseys as their home kit: Tottenham Hotspur (18th), Bolton Wanderers (19th) and Derby County (20th).

❧ WHEN THREE BECAME TWO ❧

The 1995–96 season was the first since the Premiership began three years earlier in which only two sides were promoted from the First Division, Middlesbrough as champions and play-off winners Bolton Wanderers.

❧ IF ONLY ❧

In 1992–93, Blackburn Rovers ended the inaugural Premiership season in fourth place, but they might have finished higher had Alan Shearer not been ruled out of action in December after scoring 16 goals in his first 21 league appearances. His knee injury kept him out of action until the following season.

❧ A MARK OF RESPECT FOR PRINCESS DI ❧

On 31 August 1997, the Premiership game between Liverpool and Newcastle United was postponed as a mark of respect for Diana, Princess of Wales, who had died early that morning in a car crash in Paris. On 6 September, the day of her funeral, all Premiership and Football League matches were postponed.

❧ THE GREAT DANE ❧

Peter Schmeichel was the first player to win the Premier League, FA Cup, League Cup, Charity Shield, UEFA Champions League, UEFA Super Cup (all with Manchester United), Intertoto Cup (with Aston Villa) and the European Championships (with Denmark).

❧ THE CUP KINGS ❧

In the process of winning the Treble in 1998–99, Manchester United also won their third domestic Double (after those of 1993–94 and 1995–96), while their 2–0 FA Cup final win over Newcastle United at Wembley was a record 10th win for a club in the competition.

✺ A SEASON OF FAMOUS RETIREMENTS ✺

Spring 2013 saw the end of an era in Premiership history with the retirements of a number of legends, all of whom have connections with England's north-west.

Sir Alex Ferguson – the biggest name and arguably the most influential man in the 21 years of the Premiership – stepped aside as Manchester United manager after winning his 13th Premier League title. The 71-year-old was replaced by Everton manager David Moyes after managing exactly 1,500 matches for the Reds since joining the club in November 1986, five-and-a-half seasons before the birth of the Premiership.

David Beckham – England's most capped outfield player with 115 – retired after winning championships in England (Manchester United), Spain (Real Madrid), United States (LA Galaxy) and France (Paris St Germain), the first English footballer to win league titles in four different countries.

Michael Owen – who scored 40 goals in 88 appearances for his country – might have become England's all-time leading goalscorer if he had not suffered a number of injuries. The most damaging of these was the knee injury he sustained during the 2006 FIFA World Cup. His club career took in Liverpool, Real Madrid, Newcastle United, Manchester United and Stoke City.

Jamie Carragher – a loyal one-club man – hung up his boots after 736 apearances in all competitions for Liverpool and 38 England caps. He scored on his second appearance, but managed just two more in his next 506 Premiership matches.

Phil Neville – Everton's club captain in 2012–13 – was not offered a new contract for 2013–14 and decided to hang up his boots. Neville, the younger brother of Gary, won 59 caps for England and is unusual in that he made more than 300 appearances for two clubs (303 for Everton and 389 for Manchester United).

✺ GUNNERS BEGIN TO FIRE ✺

In 1996–97, in his first full season as the manager of the Gunners, Arsene Wenger took Arsenal to third place in the Premiership.

✺ AWAY-DAY REVELLERS ✺

On their way to winning the Double in 2001–02, Arsenal were the only side not to lose a Premiership match away from home during the whole season and to score in all 38 Premiership matches.

❧ ARSENE WENGER OBE ☙

Arsene Wenger was born in Strasbourg, France, on 22 October 1949. Compared to his managerial career, however, his playing career was modest. He played as a defender for various amateur clubs while studying at Strasbourg's Robert Schuman University, obtaining a Masters degree in economics. After turning pro in 1978 he played for Strasbourg 12 times, including a UEFA Cup game, before obtaining a manager's diploma and being appointed coach of Strasbourg's youth team.

In 1984, Nancy gave Wenger his first taste of management, but he failed to turn the team's fortunes around and they were relegated to Ligue 2 in 1986–87. He then moved on to Monaco, where he enjoyed immediate success, winning Ligue 1 in 1987–88. In 1990–91 he guided them to French Cup success and was responsible for signing high-profile players for the club, including Glenn Hoddle, Jurgen Klinsmann and George Weah. After turning down advances from Bayern Munich and the French national team, Wenger was sacked by Monaco following a poor start to the 1994–95 season. He took charge of Nagoya Grampus Eight in the Japanese J-League, where he won the Emperor's Cup and Japanese J-League Super Cup in 1996.

Wenger agreed to take charge of Arsenal in August 1996, becoming their first foreign manager, but only after ensuring that the club signed French midfielders Remi Garde and Patrick Vieira. In only his second season in charge (1997–98), Arsenal won the Double of Premier League and FA Cup and so began a long-standing rivalry with Manchester United, who won titles in 1999, 2000 and 2001, with Arsenal finishing runners-up on all three occasions. Wenger guided the Gunners to their third Double in 2001–02, their second under his charge, and although the following season United regained the Premiership crown (Arsenal, again, were runners-up), Arsenal reclaimed it in 2003–04.

Arsenal won the FA Cup in 2003 and 2005, and also reached the finals of the 2000 UEFA Cup final and 2006 UEFA Champions League final under Wenger. In 2004–05 and 2005–06 both Wenger and Sir Alex Ferguson had to take back seats as Jose Mourinho and Chelsea took the championship. Arsenal finished runners-up in 2004–05, but in the following two seasons their young side had to settle for fourth place. Arsenal often were criticized for their indiscipline early in Wenger's reign, receiving 52 red cards between 1996 and 2003, but they won the Premier League's Fair Play Award in 2004 and 2005.

Did You Know That?
Wenger was the first non-British manager to win the Premier League/ FA Cup double.

℘ STRACHAN THE SAGE ℘

Some gems from **Gordon Strachan**

Reporter: "Welcome to Southampton Football Club. Do you think you are the right man to turn things around?"

Strachan: "No. I was asked if I thought I was the right man for the job and I said no. I think they should have got George Graham because I'm useless."

Reporter: "Gordon, you must be delighted with that result?"
Strachan: "You're spot on! You can read me like a book."

Strachan: "I've got more important things to think about. I've got a yogurt to finish by today, the expiry date is today. That can be my priority rather than Augustin Delgado."

Reporter: "Gordon, can we have a quick word please?"
Strachan: "Velocity." [Strachan then walked off.]

Reporter: "So, Gordon, in what areas do you think Middlesbrough were better than you today?"
Strachan: "What areas? Mainly that big green one out there."

℘ A BAD DRIVER ℘

On 22 October 2007, Manchester City's Dietmar Hamann was banned from driving for six months and ordered to pay more than £7,000 in fines for a series of motoring offences. Hamann crashed his Porsche into a fence in Styal, Cheshire, in 2006 and drove away from the scene without reporting the incident to the police.

℘ TOP DON ℘

Prior to the start of the 1995–96 season Wimbledon sold Warren Barton to Newcastle United for £4 million, making him the most expensive defender signed by any British club.

℘ UNKNOWN TERRITORY FOR UNITED ℘

Manchester United finished third in the 2001–02 Premiership behind champions Arsenal and runners-up Liverpool. It was United's lowest-ever Premiership finish: in the nine years since the league began they had been champions seven times and runners-up twice.

☙ FINAL PREMIERSHIP TABLE 2007–2008 ❧

Pos	Team	P	W	D	L	F	A	Pts
1.	Manchester United (C)	38	27	6	5	80	22	87
2.	Chelsea	38	25	10	3	65	26	85
3.	Arsenal	38	24	11	3	74	31	83
4.	Liverpool	38	21	13	4	67	28	76
5.	Everton	38	19	8	11	55	33	65
6.	Aston Villa	38	16	12	10	71	51	60
7.	Blackburn Rovers	38	15	13	10	50	48	58
8.	Portsmouth	38	16	9	13	48	40	57
9.	Manchester City	38	15	10	13	45	53	55
10.	West Ham United	38	13	10	15	42	50	49
11.	Tottenham Hotspur	38	11	13	14	66	61	46
12.	Newcastle United	38	11	10	17	45	65	43
13.	Middlesbrough	38	10	12	17	43	54	42
14.	Wigan Athletic	38	10	10	18	34	51	40
15.	Sunderland	38	11	6	21	36	59	39
16.	Bolton Wanderers	38	9	10	19	36	54	37
17.	Fulham	38	8	12	18	38	60	36
18.	Reading (R)	38	10	6	22	41	66	36
19.	Birmingham City (R)	38	8	11	19	46	62	35
20.	Derby County (R)	38	1	8	29	20	89	11

☙ MISSING THE BLUES ❧

Birmingham City were the only club in the Premier League in 2007–08 without a single England international in their squad. Arsenal had only one, Theo Walcott.

☙ A LOT OF GRASS TO COVER ❧

Manchester City played on the largest pitch in the 2012–13 Premier League. Etihad Stadium measured 116½ x 78 yards (8,932 yards²). Upton Park, West Ham, was the smallest, 110 x 70 yards (7,700 yards²).

☙ PREMIERSHIP TALK (26) ❧

"He was certainly full of it, calling me 'Boss' and 'Big Man' when we had our post-match drink after the first leg. But it would help if his greetings were accompanied by a decent glass of wine. What he gave me was paint-stripper."
Sir Alex Ferguson on Jose Mourinho

☙ GIGGS REACHES 1,000 ❧

Ryan Giggs became the third English professional footballer to appear in 1,000 matches, but the first to do so only in the top division. The Welsh legend represented his country 64 times at full international level and played in all four of Team GB's London 2012 Olympic Games matches. Giggs is unlikely to match Tony Ford's record of 931 league games – but these were all in the lower divisions – but he ended 2012–13 just 59 short of 1,000 matches for Manchester United.

☙ UNAVOIDABLE DROP ❧

On the final day of the 2007–08 season, Reading beat doomed Derby County 4–0 at Pride Park and Birmingham City saw off Blackburn Rovers 4–1 at St Andrews. Unfortunately for both, those victories were not enough to save them from relegation, as Fulham recorded a 1–0 away win at Portsmouth. Reading had needed to win by seven more goals than Fulham to send the Cottagers down on goal difference.

☙ NO MESSIAH, JUST A VERY NAUGHTY BOY ❧

Liverpool fans may hero-worship him, but Luis Suarez is looked on rather differently elsewhere, especially in the disciplinary rooms of the Football Association. The Uruguayan striker – who achieved infamy for his deliberate handball in the 2010 World Cup quarter-final aganst Ghana, for which he received a red card and one-match ban – cost the Reds £22.8 million when they bought him from Ajax in January 2011. The following season, he was suspended for eight matches for racially abusing Manchester United's Patrice Evra. Sadly in April 2013, he outdid himself when collecting a 10-match ban for biting Chelsea's Branislav Ivanovic, his second biting offence in four years.

☙ A SIGN OF THINGS TO COME ❧

On the opening weekend of the inaugural Premier League season in 1992–93, 11 players from outside UK & Ireland started for their sides. Peter Schmeichel (Denmark) Manchester United, Andrei Kanchelskis (Russia) Manchester United, Jan Stejskal (Czechoslovakia) Queens Park Rangers, Roland Nilsson (Sweden) Sheffield Wednesday, Michael Vonk (Holland) Manchester City, John Jensen (Denmark) Arsenal, Anders Limpar (Sweden) Arsenal, Hans Segers (Netherlands) Wimbledon, Tony Dorigo (Australia) Leeds United, Eric Cantona (France) Leeds United and Gunnar Halle (Norway) Oldham Athletic.

❧ MISSING IT SO BADLY ❧

Manchester United's midfielder Paul Scholes decided to retire after the Reds had lost the 2010–11 UEFA Champions League – goalkeeper Edwin van der Sar also hung up his gloves following this match – but the former England man had a change of heart during the following season and, in January 2012, returned to the Old Trafford club. He could not help the Reds to win the Premiership title that season, but he was a member of the championship squad in 2012–13 (his 11th such success, behind only team-mate Ryan Giggs on the all-time list of championship medal winners), after which he hung up his boots again

❧ LEADING PREMIERSHIP GOALSCORERS ❧

These players have scored the most goals in a Premiership season:

Pos	Goals	Player	Team	Season
1.	34	Alan Shearer	Blackburn Rovers	1994–95
=	34	Andrew Cole	Newcastle United	1993–94
3.	31	Alan Shearer	Blackburn Rovers	1993–94
=	31	Alan Shearer	Blackburn Rovers	1995–96
=	31	Cristiano Ronaldo	Manchester United	2007–08
6.	30	Kevin Phillips	Sunderland	1999–2000
=	30	Robin van Persie	Arsenal	2011–12
=	30	Thierry Henry	Arsenal	2003–04
9.	29	Didier Drogba	Chelsea	2009–10
10.	28	Robbie Fowler	Liverpool	1995–96
11.	27	Thierry Henry	Arsenal	2005–06
=	27	Wayne Rooney	Manchester United	2011–12
13.	26	Wayne Rooney	Manchester United	2009–10
=	26	Robin van Persie	Manchester United	2012–13
15.	25	Les Ferdinand	Newcastle United	1995–96
=	25	Robbie Fowler	Liverpool	1994–95
=	25	Alan Shearer	Newcastle United	1996–97
=	25	Thierry Henry	Arsenal	2004–05
=	25	Matt Le Tissier	Southampton	1993–94
=	25	Chris Sutton	Norwich City	1993–94
=	25	Ruud van Nistelrooy	Manchester United	2002–03

Did You Know That?

Robin van Persie became the man to top the goal charts for different teams in consecutive seasons when his 26 for champions Manchester United in 2012–13 followed his 30 for Arsenal the previous campaign.

☙ DOCTOR IN THE STAND ❧

A tragedy was averted at White Hart Lane on 17 March 2012, when Bolton's Congo Democratic Republic international Fabrice Muamba collapsed after suffering cardiac arrest during the Premier League club's FA Cup quarter-final against Tottenham Hostpur. Dr Andrew Deaner, a consultant cardiologist at the London Chest Hospital and Spurs season-ticket holder sitting in the stand close to the touchline, saw the incident unfold and raced onto the pitch to administer a life-saving procedure. Although Muamba's heart stopped for 78 minutes, the combined efforts of Dr Deaner and the Bolton, Tottenham and stadium medical staff, kept him alive until he was rushed to the London Chest Hospital, where full medical treatment could be given. Muamba survived, but took medical advice and retired in August 2012, by which time Bolton were playing in the Championship.

☙ ABSENT FRIEND ❧

When Carlos Tevez went home to Argentina after a spat with Manchester City manager Roberto Mancini, following the star's alleged refusal to come on as a substittute during a UEFA Champions League defeat at Bayern Munich, it started a soap opera which lasted for almost a third of the 2011–12 season. Suspended by City, Tevez said he never wanted to play for the club again, a feeling that Mancini supported as he said, "I don't think I'll select him again." However, Tevez's talent and City's desperate need for the striker in the championship race, saw burnt bridges rapidly rebuilt and Tevez played for 75 minutes of City's Premiership title-clinching 3–2 defeat of Queens Park Rangers at the Etihad on the final day of the season.

☙ TRANSFER RECORD SMASHED ❧

The January 2011 transfer window saw Chelsea smash their club record when they signed Fernando Torres from Liverpool for £50 million. "El Nino" had been a prolific scorer in his first two seasons at Anfield – he netted 65 times in 105 Reds Premiership games overall – but a series of injuries had seen his form and confidence dip. This didn't deter the defending champions Blues, who saw him as the final piece of the puzzle. Torres didn't the score the volume of goals Chelsea expected of him and they ceded the championship to Manchester United, finishing third, behind Manchester City.

❧ ARSENAL'S EUROPEAN FANTASY XI ❧

1
Jens
LEHMANN
(GERMANY)

2
Abou
DIABY
(FRANCE)

5
Per
MERTESACKER
(GERMANY)

6
Laurent
KOSCIELNY
(FRANCE)

3
Giovanni
VAN BRONCKHORST
(NETHERLANDS)

7
Marc
OVERMARS
(NETHERLANDS)

4
Patrick
VIEIRA
(FRANCE, capt.)

8
Emmanuel
PETIT
(FRANCE)

10
Dennis
BERGKAMP
(NETHERLANDS)

9
Thierry
HENRY
(FRANCE)

11
Robin
VAN PERSIE
(NETHERLANDS)

Substitutes
Manuel *ALMUNIA (Spain)* • William *GALLAS (France)* •
Robert *PIRES (France)* • John *JENSEN (Denmark)* • Cesc *FABREGAS (Spain)* •
Santi *CAZORLA (Spain)* • Freddie *LJUNGBERG (Sweden)*

Manager
Arsène *WENGER*

Did You Know That?
Arsène Wenger became the longest-serving active manager in the Premier League when Sir Alex Ferguson retired in 2013.

❧ 1,500 AND 5–5 ❧

Sir Alex Ferguson's tenure as manager of Manchester United ended in May 2013 with yet more records. After 26 years in charge, he had overseen 13 championship campaigns, all in the Premier League era, two UEFA Champions League successes, plus numerous other domestic triumphs. There had to be one last special moment, in his 1,500th match in charge of the Reds, and they – and last-day opponents West Bromwich Albion – didn't disappoint. Going into the final round of matches in the 2012–13 season, there had been a toal of 8,116 matches since the start of the 1992–93 season, but there had never been a 5–5 draw until this match at the Hawthorns. Unusually the result was achieved not by a late United fightback, but one by the Baggies, who scored three times in the last eight minutes to snatch a draw.

⚜ FINAL PREMIERSHIP TABLE 2008–2009 ⚜

Pos	Team	P	W	D	L	F	A	Pts
1.	Manchester United (C)	38	28	6	4	68	24	90
2.	Liverpool	38	25	11	2	77	27	86
3.	Chelsea	38	25	8	5	68	24	83
4.	Arsenal	38	20	12	6	68	37	72
5.	Everton	38	17	12	9	55	37	63
6.	Aston Villa	38	17	11	10	54	48	62
7.	Fulham	38	14	11	13	39	34	53
8.	Tottenham Hotspur	38	14	9	15	45	45	51
9.	West Ham United	38	14	9	15	42	45	51
10.	Manchester City	38	15	5	18	58	50	50
11.	Wigan Athletic	38	12	9	17	34	45	45
12.	Stoke City	38	12	9	17	38	55	45
13.	Bolton Wanderers	38	11	8	19	41	53	41
14.	Portsmouth	38	10	11	17	38	57	41
15.	Blackburn Rovers	38	10	11	17	40	60	41
16.	Sunderland	38	9	9	20	34	54	36
17.	Hull City	38	8	11	19	39	64	35
18.	Newcastle United (R)	38	7	13	18	40	59	34
19.	Middlesbrough (R)	38	7	11	20	28	57	32
20.	West Bromwich Albion (R)	38	8	8	22	36	67	32

⚜ OH DEAR! ⚜

Entering the 2011–12 season, Jamie Carragher had the unfortunate record of having scored more goals against Liverpool than any other active player in the Premier League. This is because, the former England international, who retired in May 2013, spent his entire career as a Liverpool player. However, his eight career own goals in all competitions – he scored only four at the right end in more than 700 appearances – is not the Premiership record. That dubious honour belongs to Irish defender Richard Dunne, who beat his own goalkeeper ten times in 451 Premiership matches for Everton, Manchester City and Aston Villa between 1997 and 2012.

⚜ PREMIERSHIP TALK (27) ⚜

"Everybody is interim, because after you there is another one. In this case they didn't have anyone so why did they put interim?"
Rafa Benitez, the clearly rankled "interim" Chelsea manager, in February 2013

ৡ GARETH BALE ৡ

Gareth Bale was born in Cardiff on 16 July 1989. He went to Whitchurch High School in Cardiff, where he was in the same year as Wales and British & Irish Lions rugby union captain Sam Warburton and Wales rugby league winger Elliott Kear. Two weeks before his 16th birthday, he made one of the most important and best decisions of his life, signing for Southampton. The Saints' youth development policy is in the top two or three in England as the success of Alan Shearer, Matt Le Tissier, Theo Walcott and Alex Oxlade-Chamberlain proves – Southampton fans wish all had played for the club at the height of their powers.

He made his debut for the Saints on 16 April 2006, three months short of his 17th birthday. Gareth played just twice that season – both 2–0 home wins – but scored his first senior goal on the opening day of the 2006–07 season. It was a breakthrough year for Gareth, who made his full international debut for Wales aged 17 years and 46 days, in a 2–0 defeat against Brazil at White Hart Lane. Less than two weeks after the end of that season, Tottenham Hotspur paid an initial £5 million to bring him to North London (the fee was eventually £7 million), thwarting rivals Arsenal, who were also interested in his signature.

Gareth suffered a season-ending injury in his eighth league appearance in December 2007, and was converted to a left-back by Juande Ramos, who was dismissed in October 2008. Harry Redknapp replaced Ramos, but kept him in the defensive role until Benoit Assou-Ekotto took his place in January. Off-season surgery delayed his return until September 2009 and he became a first-team regular in January 2010, earning the Barclays Player of the Month award that April. In 2010–11, Gareth's career took off. With the security of a new four-year contract and freedom to play further forward, he thrived and, on the night of 20 October, Gareth Bale moved into the football stratosphere with a stunning hat-trick in the San Siro Stadium, Milan, against Internazionale in the Champions League.

Suddenly he was a superstar and goals – many of them spectacular – flowed, as did accolades. PFA Young Player of the Year (2013), PFA Player of the Year (2011 and 2013), FWA Footballer of the Year (2013), have all ended up in his trophy cabinet. In 2012, he scored all of the three goals Wales registered and also represented Great Britain at the London Olympic Games. And, most judges agree, Gareth's best is yet to come.

Did You Know That?
On 26 September 2009, Gareth Bale won his first Premier League match. He had already appeared in a record 24 league matches for Spurs without once tasting victory.

⚡ SEEING YELLOW ⚡

Of the seven clubs to contest all 21 Premiership seasons, Liverpool, with 976, are the only one not to have received 1,000 yellow cards. Blackburn Rovers have the highest average of bookings with 1,090 in 18 seasons (60.56), but the five most cautioned teams are:

Team	Seasons	Yellow cards	Average
Chelsea	21	1,235	58.81
Everton	21	1,178	56.10
Arsenal	21	1,149	54.71
Tottenham Hotspur	21	1,121	53.38
Aston Villa	21	1,104	52.57

⚡ CRAZY COMEBACK ⚡

When Arsenal raced into a 4–0 lead against Newcastle United in the first 26 minutes at St James Park on 5 February 2011 (Theo Walcott, Johan Djourou and Robin Van Persie, twice, the men of target), the natives were somewhat restless and many walked out. They missed the greatest comeback in Premier League history as, helped by Abou Diaby's red-card in the 50th minute, the Gunners collapsed. Joey Barton pulled a goal back with a penalty after 63 minutes and Leon Best made it 4–2 with 15 minutes to go. A second Barton penalty, eight minutes later, got Arsenal nerves jangling and the comback was completed in the 87th minute when Cheik Tiote scored.

⚡ ROAD WOES ⚡

In the Premiership's 21 seasons, six clubs have gone through an entire campaign without an away victory: Leeds United in 1992–93, Coventry City (1999–2000), Wolverhampton Wanderers (2003–04), Norwich City (2004–05), Derby County (2007–08) and Hull City (2009–10). The Leeds statistic is the most remarkable: they were the defending champions, albeit of the old First Division; United played a 42-game schedule as opposed to the present-day 38; and the Yorkshiremen weren't relegated, finishing 17th.

⚡ MISSING IN ACTION ⚡

Only two former Football League champions have yet to play in the Premier League: Huddersfield Town (champions in 1923–24, 1924–25 and 1925–26) and Preston North End (1888–89 and 1889–90).

☙ FINAL PREMIERSHIP TABLE 2009–2010 ❧

Pos	Team	P	W	D	L	F	A	Pts
1.	Chelsea (C)	38	27	5	6	103	32	86
2.	Manchester United	38	27	4	7	86	28	85
3.	Arsenal	38	23	6	9	83	41	75
4.	Tottenham Hotspur	38	21	7	10	67	41	70
5.	Manchester City	38	18	13	7	73	45	67
6.	Aston Villa	38	17	13	8	52	39	64
7.	Liverpool	38	18	9	11	61	35	63
8.	Everton	38	16	13	9	60	49	61
9.	Birmingham City	38	13	11	14	38	47	50
10.	Blackburn Rovers	38	13	11	14	41	55	50
11.	Stoke City	38	11	14	13	34	48	47
12.	Fulham	38	12	10	16	39	46	46
13.	Sunderland	38	11	11	16	48	56	44
14.	Bolton Wanderers	38	10	9	19	42	67	39
15.	Wolverhampton Wanderers	38	9	11	18	32	56	38
16.	Wigan Athletic	38	9	9	20	37	79	36
17.	West Ham United	38	8	11	19	47	66	35
18.	Burnley (R)	38	8	6	24	42	82	30
19.	Hull City (R)	38	6	12	20	34	75	30
20.	Portsmouth (R)	38	7	7	24	34	66	19*

* Portsmouth deducted 9 points for entering Administration.

☙ ARSENAL GO GOAL CRAZY ❧

The most goals scored in the second half of a Premiership match is eight, when Arsenal and Newcastle United met at The Emirates on 22 December 2012. Theo Walcott's 20th-minute opener was cancelled out by Demba Ba just before the interval. Alex Oxlade-Chamberlain restored Arsenal's lead, only for Sylvain Marveaux to level matters. As the comic-cuts defending continued, Lukas Podolski made it 3–2, but Ba grabbed his second five minutes later. Thereafter it was all Arsenal as Walcott scored twice more to complete a hat-trick and Olivier Giroud, a 74th-minute substitute, also scored twice – and missed a sitter deep in stoppage time. This came a few weeks after Arsenal shared 19 goals in two matches with Reading, both at Madjeski Stadium. A new Carling Cup record for a single match was set as the Gunners triumphed 7–5 after extra-time (Walcott getting another hat-trick), this after they had trailed 4–2 in the 89th minute. By comparison, the Gunners' 5–2 Premier League win, six weeks later (Santi Cazorla grabbing three), was almost mundane.

✄ HAND-SHAKE ROWS ✄

Pre-match handshakes are part of modern football, a number of high-profile 2011–12 Premier League matches attracted more newsprint of photographs than the action which followed:

John Terry and Wayne Bridge: Once Chelsea team-mates, Bridge could be excused from shaking his former skipper's hand when it was revealed that Terry had an affair with Bridge's former partner.

Patrice Evra and Luis Suarez: Evra had been the victim of racial abuse by Suarez when Liverpool and Manchester United met for the first time that season – for which he was suspended eight matches. There was no handshake in the return match.

John Terry and Rio and Anton Ferdinand: Terry got in hot water – and had to answer a court case – in another racial abuse incident, this one with QPR's Anton Ferdinand. Although found not guilty by a judge, the FA suspended Terry for six matches and neither Anton nor brother Rio Ferdinand acknowledged Terry later in the season.

✄ SHORT AND NOT SO SWEET ✄

Caretaker managers, aka interim managers, have become all the rage in the Premier League, but the shortest managerial term of a "permanent" appointment was 41 days, by Charlton Athletic's Les Reed. He was in charge from 14 November to 24 December 2006.

✄ THE 500 CLUB ✄

On the last day of the 2012–13 season, and in the final match of his storied career, Paul Scholes of Manchester United became the 10th player to appear in 500 Premier League matches. Here is the list:

Player	Apps	Span
Ryan Giggs	619	1992–date
David James	573	1992–2010
Frank Lampard	560	1996–date
Gary Speed	535	1992–2008
Emile Heskey	516	1996–2012
Jamie Carragher	508	1997–2013
Philip Neville	505	1995–2013
Mark Schwarzer	504	1996–date
Sol Campbell	503	1992–2011
Paul Scholes	500	1994–2013

♞ PREMIERSHIP TALK (28) ♚

"We did not expect miracles overnight."
John Henry, Liverpool FC's owner giving new manager Brendan Rogers a little bit of time.

♞ CARING AND SHARING ♚

The most goalscorers in a single Premier League match is nine, a statistic that has been seen twice. Amazingly different players scored all nine goals in Arsenal's 5–4 victory over Tottenham Hotspur at White Hart Lane on 13 November 2004, and nine men also were on target during Portsmouth's 7–4 defeat of Reading at Fratton Park on 29 September 2007. Chelsea set the record for most goalscorers for one team in a Premier League match when seven Blues players netted during their 8–0 rout of Aston Villa at Stamford Bridge on 23 December 2012: Fernando Torres, David Luiz, Branislav Ivanovic, Frank Lampard, Ramires (two), Oscar and Eden Hazard.

♞ "1–0 TO ... WELL, EVERYBODY" ♚

Although statistics show that the most common scoreline in football is a 2–1 win, that is not the case in the Premier League. In the 8,126 matches since August 1992, there have been 1,482 1–0 victories, 18.23 per cent of all results

♞ CARD UNHAPPY ♚

Newcastle United'a James Perch had a difficult introduction to the Premier League in 2010. Signed from Nottingham Forest, he received a yellow card in all of his first five matches. For Newcastle's next match, he couldn't offend – he was serving a suspension – and saw yellow only once more during the season. Yet to be sent off for Newcastle, Perch did, however, receive nine Premier League cautions during 2012–13.

♞ PARACHUTE PAYMENTS REWARD FUTILITY ♚

A club relegated from the Premier League from 2013 will be richly rewarded for its futility. Assuming it doesn't return, in the first two seasons it will receive £41 million in parachute payments (with a further £18 million over the two following campaigns). Put into perspective, the £41 million would pay 25 players an average of more than £15,700 per week, almost £2,250 per day, over that two-year period.

☖

⚞ FINAL PREMIERSHIP TABLE 2010–2011 ⚟

Pos	Team	P	W	D	L	F	A	Pts
1.	Manchester United (C)	38	23	11	4	78	37	80
2.	Chelsea	38	21	8	9	69	33	71
3.	Manchester City	38	21	8	9	60	33	71
4.	Arsenal	38	19	11	8	72	43	68
5.	Tottenham Hotspur	38	16	14	8	55	46	62
6.	Liverpool	38	17	7	14	59	44	58
7.	Everton	38	13	15	10	51	45	54
8.	Fulham	38	11	16	11	49	43	49
9.	Aston Villa	38	12	12	14	48	59	48
10.	Sunderland	38	12	11	15	45	56	47
11.	West Bromwich Albion	38	12	11	15	56	71	47
12.	Newcastle United	38	11	13	14	56	57	46
13.	Stoke City	38	13	7	18	46	48	46
14.	Bolton Wanderers	38	12	10	16	52	56	46
15.	Blackburn Rovers	38	11	10	17	46	59	43
16.	Wigan Athletic	38	9	15	14	40	61	42
17.	Wolverhampton Wanderers	38	11	7	20	46	66	40
18.	Birmingham City (R)	38	8	15	15	37	58	39
19.	Blackpool (R)	38	10	9	19	55	78	39
20.	West Ham United (R)	38	7	12	19	43	70	33

⚞ THE "HAPPY ONE" RETURNS ⚟

One of the worst kept secrets in the second half of the Premier League season in 2013 was Chelsea manager's position. Following the departure of Roberto Di Matteo, Rafa Benitez – to the horror of many Blues fans – was appointed "interim manager", guaranteed to end at the season's close (he became coach of Serie A Napoli). This left the way clear for Jose Mourinho, the "Special One" to return, once his Real Madrid had completed the La Liga season. On 3 June 2012, the return was made public and, in Mourinho's first press conference, he didn't call himself the 'Special One", but asked to be called the "Happy One".

⚞ BAD NEWS FALLING ⚟

Birmingham City shocked Arsenal by winning the Carling Cup in 2010–11. It guaranteed them a place in the UEFA Europa League in 2011–12, but they entered this competition as a Championship side after become the first major cup-winning Premier League club to suffer relegation from the top flight in the same season.

⚜ HALF THE LEAGUE HAVE BEEN MEMBERS ⚜

In 2013–14 Cardiff City will become the 46th different club to play in the Premer League, meaning that half of the current 92 clubs have played in the top flight since 1992–93.

⚜ SOLID DEFENDING ⚜

Wigan Athletic and Chelsea did something unique in the annals of the Premier League when they met at the DW Stadium on 21 August 2010. Neither team conceded a conrer in the whole of the 90 minutes, the only time this has happened in 21 years.

⚜ SIR ALEX'S PREMIERSHIP RECORD ⚜

The only man to be in charge of a club throughout the first 21 years of the Premiership, Sir Alex Ferguson's league record at Manchester United between 1992 and 2013 was:

P	W	D	L	F	A	Pts
810	528	168	114	1,627	703	1,752

His teams averaged 2.01 goals per game, 2.16 points per game and 83.43 points per season. United's win percentage was a highly impressive 65.19.

⚜ NOMADS NO MORE ⚜

Apart from 1931–33 and 1962–63 (when they played at the White City Stadium), Queens Park Rangers have called Loftus Road – the smallest capacity stadium in the 2012–13 Premier League – their home since 1917. However, this belies their previous nomadic history. In their first 31 seasons, they played at 12 different grounds (one of them twice). This was their trail around north-west London:

Welford's Fields (1886–88) ⚜ London Scottish FC (1888–89) ⚜
Brondesbury (1888–89) ⚜ Home Farm (1888–89) ⚜
Kensal Green (1888–89) ⚜ Gun Club (1888–89) ⚜
Wormwood Scrubs (1888–89) ⚜ Kilburn Cricket Ground (1888–89) ⚜
Kensal Rise Athletic Ground (1899–1901 and 1902–04) ⚜
Latimer Road/St Quintin Avenue (1901–02) ⚜
⚜ Royal Agricultural Society Showgrounds (1904–07) ⚜
Park Royal Ground (1907–17)

♕ FINAL PREMIERSHIP TABLE 2011–2012 ♕

Pos Team	P	W	D	L	F	A	Pts
1. Manchester City (C)	38	28	5	5	93	29	89
2. Manchester United	38	28	5	5	89	33	89
3. Arsenal	38	21	7	10	74	49	70
4. Tottenham Hotspur	38	20	9	9	66	41	69
5. Newcastle United	38	19	8	11	56	51	65
6. Chelsea	38	18	10	10	65	46	64
7. Everton	38	15	11	12	50	40	56
8. Liverpool	38	14	10	14	47	40	52
9. Fulham	38	14	10	14	48	51	52
10. West Bromwich Albion	38	13	8	17	45	52	47
11. Swansea City	38	12	11	15	44	51	47
12. Norwich City	38	12	11	15	52	66	47
13. Sunderland	38	11	12	15	45	46	45
14. Stoke City	38	11	12	15	36	53	45
15. Wigan Athletic	38	11	10	17	42	62	43
16. Aston Villa	38	7	17	14	37	53	38
17. Queens Park Rangers	38	10	7	21	43	66	37
18. Bolton Wanderers (R)	38	10	6	22	46	77	36
19. Blackburn Rovers (R)	38	8	7	23	48	78	31
20. Wolverhampton Wanderers (R)	38	5	10	23	40	82	25

♕ THE YELLOW PERIL ♕

Kevin Davies set an unwanted record on 11 February 2012. The former Southampton, Blackburn Rovers and England striker became the first player to receive 100 yellow cards in the Premiership when he was booked playing for Bolton Wanderers against Wigan Athletic.

♕ 50 NOT OUT♕

The 2011–12 season saw Liverpool celebrate their 50th consecutive campaign in the First Division/Premier League, during which time they won the title 13 times, but not since 1990.

♕ CENTENARY LIONS ♕

Two players made their 100th appearance for England in 2012–13. The captain, Steven Gerrard, earned his 100th cap on 14 November 2012 in a 4–2 defeat in Sweden. Then, on 6 February 2013, Ashley Cole reached the landmark in a 2–1 victory over Brazil at Wembley.

♘ 10 YOUNGEST PREMIERSHIP GOALSCORERS ♘

When Raheem Sterling of Liverpool scored the only goal against Reading in October 2012, he became not only the club's second-youngest goalscorer in the Premier League and the eighth-youngest in the division's 21-year history, but also one of the first players born after the birth of the League to score in it (Alex Oxlade-Chamberlain is another). Here are the 10 youngest Premier League goalscorers:

Age	Player	For	Against	Date
16/270	James Vaughan	Everton	Crystal Palace	10/04/2005
16/355	James Milner	Leeds Utd	Sunderland	26/12/2002
16/360	Wayne Rooney	Everton	Arsenal	19/10/2002
17/113	Cesc Fabregas	Arsenal	Blackburn R	25/08/2004
17/144	Michael Owen	Liverpool	Wimbledon	06/05/1997
17/166	Andy Turner	Tottenham	Everton	05/09/1992
17/227	Federico Macheda	Man United	Aston Villa	05/04/2009
17/316	Raheem Sterling	Liverpool	Reading	27/10/2012
17/342	Mikael Forssell	Chelsea	Nottingham F	20/02/1999
17/344	Danny Cadamarteri	Everton	Barnsley	20/09/1997

♘ SQUEAKY BUM TIME ♘

The phrase "squeaky bum time", first attributed to Sir Alex Ferguson in 1993, describes the nerve-jangling end-of-season run-in. It soon became part of football jargon but it received official recognition in 2005, when the phrase was included in the *Collins English Dictionary*.

♘ IT HAS BEEN A LONG, LONG TIME ♘

No club in the top four divisions of English football entering the 2013–14 season had the same manager as was in charge when Arsenal last won a trophy – with one notable exception. Arsène Wenger was in charge of the Gunners when they lifted the 2005 FA Cup – before the rebuilding of Wembley Stadium was complete – and the Frenchman was still the Gunners' boss in June 2013.

♘ PREMIERSHIP TALK (29) ♘

"A rare breed and it's been a privilege to play alongside, room with and be big mates with one of football's real men."
Michael Owen, on his former Liverpool and England teammate Jamie Carragher, who retired in 2013

✵ FINAL PREMIERSHIP TABLE 2012–2013 ✵

Pos	Team	P	W	D	L	F	A	Pts
1	Manchester United (C)	38	28	5	5	86	43	89
2	Manchester City	38	23	9	6	66	34	78
3	Chelsea	38	22	9	7	75	39	75
4	Arsenal	38	21	10	7	72	37	73
5	Tottenham Hotspur	38	21	9	8	66	46	72
6	Everton	38	16	15	7	55	40	63
7	Liverpool	38	16	13	9	71	43	61
8	West Bromwich Albion	38	14	7	17	53	57	49
9	Swansea City	38	11	13	14	47	51	-46
10	West Ham United	38	12	10	16	45	53	-46
11	Norwich City	38	10	14	14	41	58	44
12	Fulham	38	11	10	17	50	60	41
13	Stoke City	38	9	15	14	34	45	42
14	Southampton	38	9	14	15	49	60	41
15	Aston Villa	38	10	11	17	47	69	41
16	Newcastle United	38	11	8	19	45	68	41
17	Sunderland	38	9	12	17	41	54	39
18	Wigan Athletic (R)	38	9	9	20	47	73	36
19	Reading (R)	38	6	10	22	43	73	28
20	Queens Park Rangers (R)	38	4	13	21	30	60	25

✵ TOWNS CRYING ✵

Blackburn Rovers, in the 1994–95 season, is the only team from a town – as opposed to a city (London and Manchester being the only two) – to have had champions of the Premier League. In 2013–14, only the town of West Bromwich will play in the Premier League. Ipswich was the last club with the Town suffix to win the top flight title and that was in 1961–62.

✵ SIR ALEX FERGUSON – CUP COLLECTOR ✵

In 27 seasons at Old Trafford 1986–2013, Sir Alex Ferguson won an amazing 38 trophies. This is the complete list
:

13 FA Premier League ✵ 1 FIFA World Club Cup ✵
2 UEFA Champions League ✵ 1 Intercontinental Cup ✵
1 UEFA Super Cup ✵ 1 European Cup-winners' Cup ✵
5 FA Cup ✵ 4 Football League Cup ✵
10 FA Charity/Community Shield